Ernest Geldart

A manual of church decoration and symbolism

Ernest Geldart
A manual of church decoration and symbolism
ISBN/EAN: 9783337259747

Printed in Europe, USA, Canada, Australia, Japan

Cover: Foto ©Lupo / pixelio.de

More available books at **www.hansebooks.com**

By

THE REV. ERNEST GELDART,
Rector of Little Braxted.

CONTAINING DIRECTIONS AND ADVICE TO THOSE
WHO DESIRE WORTHILY TO DECK THE CHURCH
AT THE VARIOUS SEASONS OF THE YEAR:

❖ also ❖

THE EXPLANATION AND THE HISTORY OF THE
SYMBOLS AND EMBLEMS OF RELIGION.

With LII. PLATES AND MANY ILLUSTRATIONS
By the AUTHOR.

A. R. MOWBRAY & CO.
OXFORD: 106, S. Aldate's Street;
LONDON: 64 and 65, Farringdon Street, E.C.
1899.

ERRATA.

Page 92, line 13, *for* Ημετερ Cοσωτηρ *read* Ημετερος Cωτηρ.
„ 96, line 21, *for* Patriachal *read* Patriarchal.
„ 105, line 34, *for* signum *read* lignum.

PREFACE.

READER,

You have in your hands the fruit of five-and-thirty years of my work in one field of GOD'S fair earth. Of its unripeness and poor savour you cannot be as conscious as am I.

All that can be hoped, is that you may be by it inclined to a more intelligent cultivation of that branch of the Tree of Knowledge, whence, at the call of GOD, Bezaleel and Aholiab plucked the pomegranates, to deck His Tabernacle among men.

Hence, too, unnumbered thousands after them, have gathered the ever-ripening fruit, for the glorious service of the Sanctuary.

I count not myself, by any means, to have apprehended the full increase of the ages; nor, while entering into the labours of others, to have done aught but "glean after them." For this, like Ruth, may I "not be rebuked," since I have tried only to take what lies ready to any man's hand.

Whatsoever it is, I only offer to you what, in all honesty, I have (on the preceding page) already offered to the Giver of all good work, and the Gracious Receiver of all well-meant labour.

Ad te domine
levavi oculos.

ACKNOWLEDGMENT.

My indebtedness to others is well nigh infinite. "What hast thou that thou hast not received?" is ever true, but truest perhaps of all, in matters of art. "Other men laboured, and we have entered into their labours." To write even such a book as that which you, my reader, have in your hands, would have been a hopeless task to any one man, had he not the benefit of his predecessors' work.

Most gratefully do I give thanks to all who have gone before me, whose harvests I have gleaned.

From nineteen centuries of Christian art it would be strange if nothing were gathered; but the field is too wide, and the task too great for one; and I have taken from the basket and the store of many.

It is impossible to give a full acknowledgment of this indebtedness, but at least I can mention a few of those whose greater labours have lightened my lesser toil.

Foremost in the list of modern writers, Husenbeth must be mentioned. His *Emblems of the Saints* is the storehouse to which I have gone oftenest, and from which I have gathered most. Didron's *Christian Iconography*, perhaps, comes next; but besides these two books, I have consulted many others: Parker's *Calendar of the Prayer Book;* Mrs. Jameson's *Sacred and Legendary Art;* Smith's *Dictionary of Christian Antiquities;* Boutell's *Heraldry;* Walcot's *Dictionary of Archaeology;* Brand's *Popular Antiquities;* Twining's *Christian Symbolism;* Viollet le Duc's *Dictionary;* Mazot's *Tableau de la Croix;* Creeny's *Brasses of Europe;* the *Ecclesiologist* of the Camden Society; Palmer's *Early Christian Symbolism,* and a score of other books, have frequently been referred to.

Nor must I omit to state that many parts of the chapters on Temporary Decoration are, more or less, borrowed from a book edited by me in 1882, for the then existing firm of Cox, Sons, & Co., as in *that* book they were chiefly taken from a former book, published many years ago by Mr. E. Y. Cox.

Several of the illustrations are reproduced from Didron, and others from various standard works: but the majority of the drawings are original, and are the result of more than thirty years' study of ancient work at home and abroad.

For the beautiful frontispiece, I am indebted to Mr. Percy Bacon, of the firm of Bacon Brothers, 11, Newman Street, Oxford Street, W. These artists have for several years executed all the carved and painted work which I have designed as architect.

For the rest, most sincerely I acknowledge myself (consciously or unconsciously) a plagiarist and a borrower. Had it been otherwise, this book would have been, if more "my own," a "still poorer thing."

✠

deo

omnium visibilium auctori

qui

oculos et manus

mihi dedit

opusculum

hoc

refero.

✠

CONTENTS.

PART I.

CHAPTER I.

Of decoration generally, its use and abuse; the danger of individualism; floral decoration in pre-Christian and mediaeval times; historical notes; reference to parish accounts, etc. . . . . 1—6

CHAPTER II.

The principles of decoration applied: (*a*) it should be unobnoxious; (*b*) harmless to the fabric; (*c*) it should not obscure permanent ornament; (*d*) it should not be discordant; (*e*) it should be constructionally true; (*f*) it should be free from sameness; (*g*) it should not be extravagant; (*h*) nor disproportionate; (*i*) it should avoid scandal; (*k*) irreverence; (*l*) it should be methodical . . 7—20

CHAPTER III.

Of wreaths and garlands; materials required; methods of making; examples of the right and wrong way of applying such things; filling in of blank spaces; hanging festoons; emblematical devices in evergreen work; ironmongery and water troughs . . . . 21—32

CHAPTER IV.

Floral decoration; cut flowers and everlastings; mixture of evergreens and flowers; flowers appropriate to certain days; decorative use of lights . . . 33—39

CHAPTER V.

Of colours; their liturgical and symbolic signification; of numbers and geometrical forms . . . . 40—43

CHAPTER VI.

Of temporary structures, screens, font-covers, etc.; their value as tentative experiments; the limitations of their usefulness . . . . . 44—48

CHAPTER VII.

Of banners and flags; the method of making such things in silk, canvas, or embroidery; of painted banners and dossals . . . . . 49—53

CHAPTER VIII.

On the use of texts as permanent decorations; on their employment at various seasons; their use as memorials; the simplicity of such inscriptions in ancient times; on chronograms . . . . 54—67

CHAPTER IX.

A selection of texts for the seasons of the year, and several occasions; texts suitable for the various parts of the Church . . . . . 68—74

x   Contents.

PART II.

CHAPTER X.

Of emblems generally; their different nature, whether symbolical, doctrinal, metaphorical, historical, official, representative, "canting," or traditional; an alphabetical list of such emblems, with a few examples of saints' names associated therewith . . . . 75—82

CHAPTER XI.

Of the Ever-blessed Trinity; absence of early representations; later anthropomorphism; description of examples illustrated; the Three Persons shown separately . . . . 83—89

CHAPTER XII.

Of the Holy Name; its early spelling; the contractions which have produced the familiar "monograms;" fanciful interpretations; description of examples illustrated . . . . 90—95

CHAPTER XIII.

Other emblems of our Lord; their history and character at various times: (1) the Agnus Dei; (2) the Alpha and Omega; (3) the anchor; (4) the cross; (5) the candlestick; (6) the fish and *vesica;* (7) the hand; (8) the lion; (9) the peacock; (10) the pelican; (11) the phœnix; (12) the "trophies" or emblems of the passion; (13) the pomegranate; (14) the rose; (15) the *fleur de lys* and other signs of our Lady; (16) the star; (17) the sun; (18) the ship or ark; (19) the Blessed Sacrament; (20) the Good Shepherd; (21) the whale; (22) the wise men's offerings . . . . 96—127

CHAPTER XIV.

Of the holy Angels; their choirs and orders; traces of these in the liturgy; Dionysius the Areopagite, his classification accepted generally by the Church; the *archangels*—four or seven? Byzantine manual for painters, its rules and directions . . . . 128—133

CHAPTER XV.

The four Evangelists; their "symbols;" the arrangement and order of these when grouped together; occasional appropriation of their symbols to doctors of the Church, or the greater prophets . . . . 134—138

CHAPTER XVI.

The holy Apostles; the twelve foundations; who were the twelve? articles of the Creed attributed to each several Apostle; positions in which their images or pictures are found . . . . 139—144

CHAPTER XVII.

The twelve Prophets; Old or New Testament prophets referred to in Acts xiii. 1, and the *Te Deum?* emblems of prophets and patriarchs 145

CHAPTER XVIII.

The Calendar: the English Prayer Book supplemented from various sources: the modern Roman and old English Calendars in parallel columns . . 146—153

Contents.

CHAPTER XIX.

The names of the saints arranged alphabetically, with their traditional emblems; many saints undistinguished or indistinguishable . . . . . . 154—161

CHAPTER XX.

The aureole and nimbus; not Christian in origin; different forms, circular and otherwise . . . . 162—166

CHAPTER XXI.

The heraldry of the shield; the elementary laws of blazonry; description of the shield and its divisions; tinctures, furs, lines, ordinaries, subordinaries, etc. . 167—173

CHAPTER XXII.

The form of the shield; examples of ancient shields, dating from the eleventh to the sixteenth century; cautions as to the position of shields when used decoratively . . . . 174—177

CHAPTER XXIII.

The arms and emblems of the saints; description of plates illustrating the traditional coats of arms, and the better known emblems . . . . . 178—195

CHAPTER XXIV.

The arms of the English Bishoprics . . . . . . 196—200

CHAPTER XXV.

The crown: its development illustrated by many examples, thirty-four in all . 201—203

CHAPTER XXVI.

The mitre: its shape and gradually increasing magnificence; its fate on passing from the bishops' heads to the hands of the coach-builder . . . 204—206

OTHER WORKS BY THE SAME AUTHOR.

Missa de Sanctis.
A Plainsong Service.   Organ Part, 2/-;   Voice Part, 3d.

Missa Dominica.
Another Service.   Organ Part, 6d.;   Voice Part, 1½d.

NOVELLO, BERNER STREET.

Brief Explanation of the Ceremonies of the Holy Eucharist.
Adapted from the Latin of Hazé.   Price, 1/-   *(Of the Author.)*

Three Hymns with Plainsong Melodies.
Price 3d.   *(Of the Author.)*

A Manual of
Church Decoration and Symbolism.

CHAPTER I.

Of Decoration generally.

(Ancient and Modern: Passing and Permanent.)

"Ask counsel of both times," said Lord Bacon; "of the old time what is *best*, of the new time what is *fittest*."

This admirable statement of a general truth unhappily needs a qualification ere it can be applied all round.

In fact the author, in another place, himself supplies one:

"As the births of living creatures at first are ill-shapen, so are all innovations which are the birth of Time." *

The subject of which the present book largely treats, must, alas! fall under this condemnation—an innovation, most certainly, and an ill-shapen one too!

Church Decoration, as it is now understood—the appropriate garnishing to suit the varying season of the year—is but a thing of yesterday, and it has all the faults and failings of the over-young: too often ugly, nearly always over-bearing, assertive, noisy, and undisciplined—mischievous.

Yet we will accept the responsibility laid on us to-day in that our zeal has given birth to this offspring of the new time. We must try to educate it and keep it within due bounds, lest, like Jeshurun, it wax too fat and kick too lustily.

The old time was best, no doubt, and we may scarce ever hope to see our sanctuaries ablaze with glory and beauty as they were throughout this land of England long ago.

Scarce a tiny village Church was undecorated and unpainted in the days when God's House was the brightest, as well as the best of all the dwellings round it.

Scarce such a Church *now*, if it has not passed through the mill of restoration, but has traces of colour left on the walls, perhaps preserved beneath the snowy

---

* Essays xxiv. 1625.

winding-sheet of Churchwardens' whitewash, ready to spring forth again to gladden us of to-day who have eyes to see the beauties that our fathers had forgotten ; perchance, still showing in faded patches here and there, but still existing.

Yes; the old time was best! When wall, and beam, and window, and rafter were decorated with gold and colour as well as carved work.

Then the decking of the sanctuary was simple : a few flowers, a wreath or two of box and yew, a garland of fresh leaves, and sweet-smelling rushes on the floor ; each altar "decorated" with lights, and every statue with its birthday posy. Calico texts, paper banners, crystal powder, and everlasting flowers steeped in aniline dyes, and all such abominations were unknown. But, as I say, we will accept the dictum of Bacon, and presume that for us it *is* fittest to use temporary decorations more than the men of old, since "the stone out of the wall, and the beam of the timber answer" not our cry as they were used to do afore.

If then we are to decorate our Churches, the question we set ourselves to answer is rather, "How shall we do it?" than "Shall we?"

All decoration, whether permanent or temporary, has a double purpose to serve : the glory of GOD, and the edifying of His children.

The first result is assured, if whatsoever is done is the outcome of an honest and good heart ; but the latter can only be secured when good taste directs good will, so that it comes to good effect.

Our LORD, by Whom all things were made, and to Whom all things belong, cares not to distinguish between pine and oak, or bone and ivory, glass and diamonds, tin and precious gold. All things are His, and when we give Him of His own, the offering is accepted according to what we have, and not according to what we have not.

So, many a time we have to pass over with a tender hand and gentle eye excruciating abominations, the work of loving hearts, which, if we rejected, some poor soul would be discouraged from ever after attempting to do anything for the House of the LORD, and the weak would be turned out of the way. We must be patient with newborn zeal, and not mock at its ugliness.

Nevertheless, we cannot allow the sanctuary to be permanently disfigured ; and no matter at what cost to private feelings, the structure, the fittings, and the ornamenting of the Church must be such as shall be worthy, or at least not too unworthy, of the House of GOD.

When one thinks of the way in which havoc has been made altogether of Westminster Abbey by funereal profanation, and how in half our Churches private "malefactors" have been allowed to erect memorials of folly, one can only pray for some godly reformation to sweep them all away.

East windows, filled with pictures of the Prodigal Son, the Blessing of Little Children, the Raising of Jairus' Daughter, the Good Samaritan, or the Giving Sight to the Blind, come to one's mind at once as the most harmless examples of incongruous vandalism.

A good lady has lost a daughter, or a doctor-husband, or a sailor-boy : forthwith the East window of the Church is made the vehicle to convey to succeeding generations *her* private griefs, and not the mystery of Redemption.

Church furniture of all sorts is, in the same way, made the opportunity of individualism. A pulpit like the one at Blankbury is stuck violently into Little Snoring because the donor always "fancied" it, and not in the least because it fits or suits the place in which it is inserted. So much is this terrible error engrained in us that we nearly all talk of "our lectern" and "our font," because, forsooth, "our money" purchased it.

No faithful guardian of a House of GOD ought to suffer misguided liberality to spoil it. No faithful son or daughter of the Church ought ever to dream of identifying any part of it with private joy or grief, or family bereavement.

Truly, nothing is more suitable than that such touchings of GOD'S hand should open ours to give of our substance towards His Church; but only in such sort that our part is lost in the whole, for the whole is "greater than its parts, and the work is great, for the palace is not for man, but GOD."

So, too, all the decoration and furnishing of a Church should have a clear and distinct congruity, the one part with the other. We should never see, for instance, carved oak benches in the nave, and "pitch pine" stalls, and a deal altar. In these æsthetic days such words would be deemed superfluous in regard to a house at Bedford Park, where peacock-blue dadoes and high-art curtains match beautifully; or at Harrow or Bushey, where the half-timbering and red tiles without, speak of a corresponding style within. We like to have everything *en suite* and "all of a piece" at home; but in Church—it seems that every man may do that which is "right in his own eyes."

Mistaken perpetrations and perpetuations of bad taste are naturally more serious than the passing show of a harvest festival or a Christmas dressing, which can be pulled down and swept away in an hour; but all bad taste is more or less enduring, and leaves a flavour and an after-taste behind, establishing a corrupt tradition, to be avoided at all pains if possible.

We will suppose, then, that our readers wish to "decorate" a Church for a festival. The purpose of this book, or part of it, is to help them in their good endeavours, and to secure that as little harm as possible may be done to the fabric of the building, or the sensibility of the cultured mind.

As already stated, the method of "dressing" a Church (to use the old country term) commonly used in the middle ages, was to strew the floor with rushes, box, yew, or even grass; to hang garlands from the roof, and on the walls, and to put candles on prickets before statues and altars, and especially to deck the rood beam in like manner.

Such decoration goes back to the earliest ages of mankind, and is certainly not *distinctively* Christian. The priest of Jove brought garlands to S. Paul, whom he mistook for his god.* The heathen of many lands decked themselves and

---

* Acts xiv. 13.

their idols with roses and wreaths of ilex, vine, and laurel at their festivals. And the chosen people of GOD were bidden, too, to observe a feast every year, and to gather " boughs of goodly trees, of palm trees, and thick trees, and willows of the brook, a statute for ever in their generations." *

This custom evidently became more than a solitary decoration once a year, for Isaiah mentions in general terms, " The fir tree, the cedar, the pine tree, and the box together, beautifying the place of the sanctuary." †

Christians, when desiring to make their worship beautiful, did not disdain to use the means at hand, nor did they think such means to be rejected merely because both Jew and Gentile had before employed them.

The *Floralia* of the heathen did not deter them from gathering GOD'S fairest works and spreading them in His House. Nor did they think to Judaize, because if their spiritual forebears had cut down branches of trees, they, too, strewed the floor with sweet-smelling boughs.

S. Jerome praises his friend Nepotian for his care of Divine worship, " using flowers of all sorts to decorate the sanctuary."

But we need not try to trace the custom through the long centuries ; suffice it to say that there is a continuous chain of evidence from the earliest ages till the present day. Prosaic parish accounts and poetic verses alike tell the same tale.

Yet we cannot fail to notice that the chief times of decoration were not so strictly "churchy" as we might be inclined to suppose. Of Christmas, May Day, and Palm Sunday (the chief outbreaks of enthusiasm), the two first were almost more externally than internally, domestically than ecclesiastically, observed.

May Day, especially, was certainly not kept as it is to-day in France, in honour of our Lady, but " going a-Maying " was rather, as Chaucer says, because

> " The season pricketh every gentle heart,
> And maketh it out of his sleep to start ;
> And saith, Arise and *do May observance*. . . ."

In fact, the clergy were rebuked by Bishop Grostete, of Lincoln, for their participation in the May sports : *Faciunt, ut audivimus, clerici ludos quos vocant* Inductionem Maii, *et* Festum Autumni. . . ."

Yet these decorations were not entirely extra-ecclesiastical, for Spenser, in 1579, says of those who went a-Maying :

> " Youths now flock in everywhere
> To gather May buskets ‡ and smelling briar,
> And home they hasten the posts to dight,
> And all the Church pillars ere daylight."

George Herbert, in the *Country Parson*, 1657, says : " Our parson takes order that the Church be swept and kept clean . . . and at great festivals strawed and stuck with boughs."

* Lev. xxiii. 40. † Isa. lx. 13. ‡ Busket is the familiar *bouquet* spelt otherwise.

Of Decoration generally.

So out of innumerable Churchwardens' accounts, the following entries may suffice to show the means employed:

S. Laurence, Reading, 1644.

p^d for Holly and Ivy, Rosemary and Bay at Christmas -	- £0 1 10
p^d for Yew . . . againt Easter - - - - - -	- 0 1 8

S. Margaret's, Westminster, 1647.

item paid for Rosemarie and Bays that was stuck about the Church at Christmas - - - - - - - £0 1 6

S. Mary Outwich, London, 1510.

p^d for Palm, box, flowers, and cakes - - - -	- iiij^d
p^d for Broom against Easter - - - - - -	- j^d

All Hallows', Staining.

item for Box and Palm on Palm Sunday - - - - ij^d

S. Mary at Hill.

Garlands Whitsunday - - - - - - - - iii^d
Three great garlands for the crosses, of roses and lavender, three dozen other garlands for the choir - - - - - £0 3 0

So, too, we have copious evidence from wills, of pious bequests to provide lamps and candles; and one interesting benefaction is recorded, as given by John Lane, of Yatton, in Somersetshire. The deceased "gent of this parish" left half an acre of ground to the poor, reserving a quantity of grass for strewing the Church at Whitsunday.

The Puritan "interval," of course, did much to break unnumbered traditions, and abolish many ancient customs. For all that, Church Decorations, and especially the use of *holly*, the red rag to the Puritan Bull, did not quite die out, for Coles, writing in 1656, says: "In some places setting up of holly, ivy, rosemary, bay, yew, etc., in Churches at Christmas is *still in use*." If such things were permitted in the *Church*, I doubt not that in Puritan *households* even worse abominations were practised; I fear me that the ungodly plum porridge and the deadly mince pie were secretly consumed, in spite of sour disfavour and penal law.

As time went on, the days of decoration got fewer and farther apart, until, in the early part of this century, Christmas was almost the *only* full-dressed time, yet the old tradition was exact, and stringently observed, that the holly should remain till Candlemas.

Rush-bearing on S. Bartholomew's Day used to be observed till recently at Donnington, in Lincolnshire, and also at Grasmere, in the English Lakes. So, too, at Warton, in Lancashire, Dr. Whitaker gives a description of the procession of rush-bearers, who, having brought their rushes to the Church, leave them there, generally "over the cancelli." *

The comparative rareness of "decorated festivals" in the past we owe, with many another dubious blessing, to Henry VIII., who, in 1536, passed an Act, ordering that henceforward no Church-days nor dedication festivals were to be held on any day except the first Sunday in October. The Act itself is too long to quote, but one cannot but be amused at the clear eye to the main chance which characterizes not it alone, but so much of the "Reformation unsettlement." Having with pious horror described the looseness of living and ill-behaviour of the frequent participators in Church-days' observances, the Act goes on to state as a climax, that such things produced not only the afore-named loose living, but "*yea, even the wasting of men's goods ! ! !*" For, it says, men would even leave the crops to rot while they went to Church.

The various extracts and references above given provide us with a fairly clear picture of the decorated Church in the times up to and even succeeding the Reformation : the floors strewn with rushes ; the pillars, or "posts," as Spenser calls them, wreathed round with garlands of leaves and flowers ; garlands, too, of box and yew suspended from the roof ; the rood decked with a wreath of flowers ; bushes and boughs of evergreen or may standing thereon, and in vacant corners of the floor ; candles and hanging lamps glimmering before the various shrines and altars ; statues garlanded and decked with pots of flowers before them ; and the sweet smell of the fresh-trodden rushes mingling with the incense—but never a whiff of the mineral oil and smoky anthracite that we so often are forced to breathe, even where care and pious use (aided by ventilation) have banished from our Churches that terrible composite odour of musty sourness that all of us inevitably associate with the Church-going of our childhood.

* *Trad. of Lancashire*, Vol. ii. p. 108.

CHAPTER II.

The Principles of Decoration and the practices arising therefrom.

THESE principles, as here stated, will probably recall to some readers the ones enunciated in *Workers together with God*.[*] My only excuse is that I cannot change my principles, and find it hard to state them except in language more or less similar to that employed when writing upon exactly the same subject.

The first canon is surely this:

I.

DECORATION SHOULD BE UNOBNOXIOUS.

A Church, after it is decorated, should be at least as fit to use as before.

A decorated Church should not hinder the officiant, nor damage his vestments.

Nor should it give physical pain or injury to priest or congregation.

Surely no one could dissent from this; or *in theory* wish to controvert or contravene such a self-evident truth. Obvious, however, as it is, a large proportion of the "decorations," falsely so called, cumber the ground, and so embarrass the clergy, that each festival, as it comes, has a dark shadow of foreboding, a "sense of impending disaster." Hope against hope of "getting through somehow" without upsetting the feelings of the decorators or lacerating our own hands, is, in many cases, the best we can look for.

The past is too sad to comfort us for the future. We have entreated for breathing and passage room before in vain; yet we venture once more to hope that when all is done we may emerge scathless.

I will ask my readers to enter with me (in imagination) a Church which has suffered "the extreme penalty" of the lawless decorator. Let it not be supposed that any *one* Church would ever combine all the horrors here depicted, or that such barbarism is universal. But sorrowful experience, and not a mere desire to say smart things, has painted the picture of this interior.

We will suppose that the ladders and trestles, the baskets, and piles of snippings have disappeared from the Church and Churchyard. On entering the door the first sensation is of darkness and unfamiliarity. "It's the *windows*—they always darken the Church!" We find the poor man's box covered with a pot

---

[*] *Workers together with God.* A Series of Papers on some of the Church's Works by some of the Church's Workers. Edited by the Rev. NATHANIEL KEYMER, M.A., Rector of Headon, Notts, and a Canon Missioner in the Diocese of Southwell. Mowbrays.

of flowers, and the only receptacle for money that meets our eyes is one "For the Decorations!" This does not appeal to us, and we turn to the font. This is for *Baptism*—according to ancient custom on Easter and Whitsun Eve, by common usage on any day, and, by the Prayer Book advice, preferably on festivals. But what do we find, save a plantation of geraniums, or a pile of pumpkins and apples, or whatever the "seasonable surroundings" may be? The flat lid, turned *upside down*, is piled with hassocks, and moss, and flowers, surmounted by a tottering cross of cotton wool and stephanotis.

Or if it is Christmas time, the font cover is a mound of cotton wool—*snow*, with little rivulets of beaded holly-berries running to the base at equal distances. In the triangular segments of the cone blaze stars of Bethlehem of gilt paper, a holly hedge of unapproachable sharpness surrounds the basin, while a gentle rain of Epsom salts has given brightness to the whole.

Or it is summer time, and there is no cover on the font—it is too warm—but instead there is a gallon or two of water, with a floating cross of arums and dead leaves, defiling the basin.

"There is a Baptism to-morrow," we remark; to which a piteous wail is raised by the decorator, "It is really *too* bad." It is!

Leaving the font we win our way as carefully as we can to the chancel-screen. In an unguarded moment we rest our hand upon the rail, and receive a pint of water down our coat-sleeve. We have overbalanced a trough, which a tin-tack was supposed to hold in position. We look at, or rather for, the screen, but its familiar lines are lost. In place of the slender mullions are huge boas of holly; the traceried panels below are filled with gilt paper, and the upper arches blocked with red flannel banners.

The lectern (an eagle, of course)* has probably a banner slung round the neck, and "choice exotics" surrounding it in paper-covered pots.

The pulpit is only to be approached with the greatest circumspection, unless the preacher desires to be unfrocked.

---

* The eagle was the *Gospel desk*, and not a choir lectern for the daily lessons. Its proper position is in the sanctuary, flanked with two standard candles.

The stairs have flower-pots on every step; the hand-rail is wreathed with holly; "the desk *must not be touched, please*," or no one knows what will happen, until, in the middle of the sermon, perhaps, the unexpected comes to pass, and a shoot of all sorts of things is precipitated into the front pew, to the delight of the choir-boys, and the indignation of the decorator.

The reading-desk has a brown paper band glued round its edges, covered with holly; on this the reader's fingers are pricked, and the "newly-presented" bookmarkers are caught, the leaves of the Prayer Book probably torn, and a few holly-berries crushed between them.

The stalls, too, often are a source of inexhaustible interest to the choir-boys, who are able to make quite a *hortus siccus* in their psalters, by collecting the loose sprays of maiden hair fern, and so forth.

The altar-rails are supposed to be a means of support to the aged and infirm. What can be more distressing to the communicants, at the most solemn moment

of reception, than to prick their wrists with holly, to find that they have knelt upon a bunch of grapes, or to feel with unavoidable self-consciousness, that their clothes are patched with cotton wool, and disfigured with crushed fruit and flowers?

The altar itself is too sad for description, and I will leave the accompanying sketch to speak for itself. I have more than once seen such a travesty of "GOD'S BOARD," and know that there is no exaggeration whatever in this terrible representation.

Turning from the actual furniture of the Church, we are struck, perhaps, as much as anything, by the gas brackets. The natural warmth of the building, and the additional heat of the burning gas, render these disfigurements more transitory than the rest, but they are bad while they last.

The columns and the arches we will look to presently, as they do not offend against the first canon. We can *use* the Church just as well, however ugly the wreaths may be. But from the windows we have a right to expect light. But nothing gives more pleasure to some decorators' hearts than to make conservatories of the window ledges, and plant out the light of heaven.

II.

DECORATION MUST BE HARMLESS TO THE FABRIC.

Never on any account should a nail (or even a tin-tack) be driven into either wood or stone.*

If you cannot make a decoration stay in its place by the law of gravitation, or by the use of string and wire, take it away and find some other place for it.

To drive nails into a rough plaster wall for the suspension of wreaths and so on, is harmless, but to break the joints of a stone or marble pulpit, to riddle the edges and split the panels of oak stalls, is not *decoration* but *desecration*.†

* That is to say, the wood and stone of which stalls or pulpit or font are made, or the *wrought stone* of doors and windows and arches.

† What could happen, for instance, to the beautiful stalls of Southwold, or to the pulpit of Holne, or that in Wendon Church, or to the lectern and screen drawn on Plates I. and II., if surrendered to the tender mercies of the decorator?

PULPIT IN WENDON CHURCH, ESSEX.
PORTION OF SCREEN, FAIRFORD.
LECTERN IN BERNE CATHEDRAL.

EXAMPLES OF THINGS INCAPABLE OF FURTHER DECORATION.

PULPIT IN HOLNE CHURCH, DEVON.

Let any one calculate the number of festivals and the number of nails driven in each time, and it may easily be judged how long it will take before the ill-used object is completely destroyed. A century of such treatment would wreck the most substantial pulpit or font in existence.

Another plan, less destructive but almost equally disfiguring, is to stick brown paper, with glue or sealing-wax, on to the window-sills, font, pulpit, stalls, or lectern, and upon this foundation to sew floral decorations. It should be unnecessary to remark that neither stone nor wood will endure the washing and scraping necessary for its removal without damage.

III.

DECORATION OF THE DECORATED IS NOT PERMISSIBLE.

Gilding the refined gold is *superfluous*, but covering up costly marble or carved oak with trumpery paper banners, or cotton wool, or shapeless bunches of greenery is *outrageous*.

A plain square font may be fairly

FONT AT CLOVELLY FONT AT DUNSFOLD FONT AT KIRKBY MISPERTON

decorated, so long as its use is not hindered, and a font cover of wire may suitably be employed if it is easily removable. So, too, a plain pulpit may have its panels filled if the decorations will stay in naturally; and its base may have both evergreens and flowers round it, provided they get in no one's way.

The examples given on pages 8, 9, and 10 will, perhaps, suffice by way of warning, and generally it will be well if this rule is accepted: "Decorate plain spaces, and leave all ornaments and details severely alone."

IV.

NEVER INTERFERE WITH THE ARCHITECTURAL LINES OF THE BUILDING.

There are always certain leading lines, both vertical and horizontal, which are part of the nature of the building itself, and if they are contradicted and traversed, the whole effect is marred: whence it follows that the greatest care must be exercised in wreathing columns or splining arches. The thick round columns of a Norman arcade may be spirally twined with evergreens, and the square reveals of the various orders of the arches may be lined with bands of box or ivy. But to twine a slender shaft with bands nearly as thick as itself is fatally destructive of its beauty.*

V.

NEVER INVENT IMPOSSIBLE FEATURES.

Arches supporting nothing, for instance, are as absurd as they are hideous. So to put an "arcade" on a blank wall, or a pointed gable where there is nothing to suggest such forms is ridiculous. On the other hand, a blank arch may

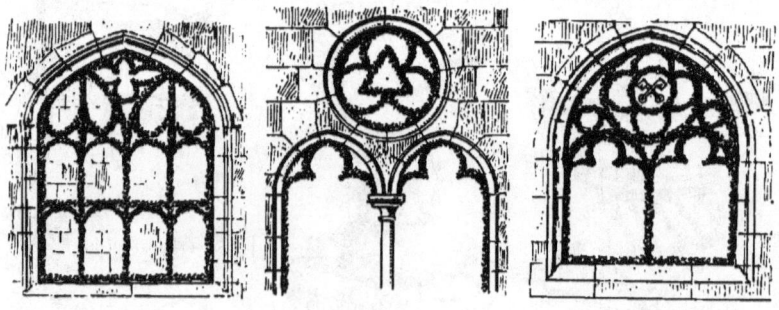

* See plate III.

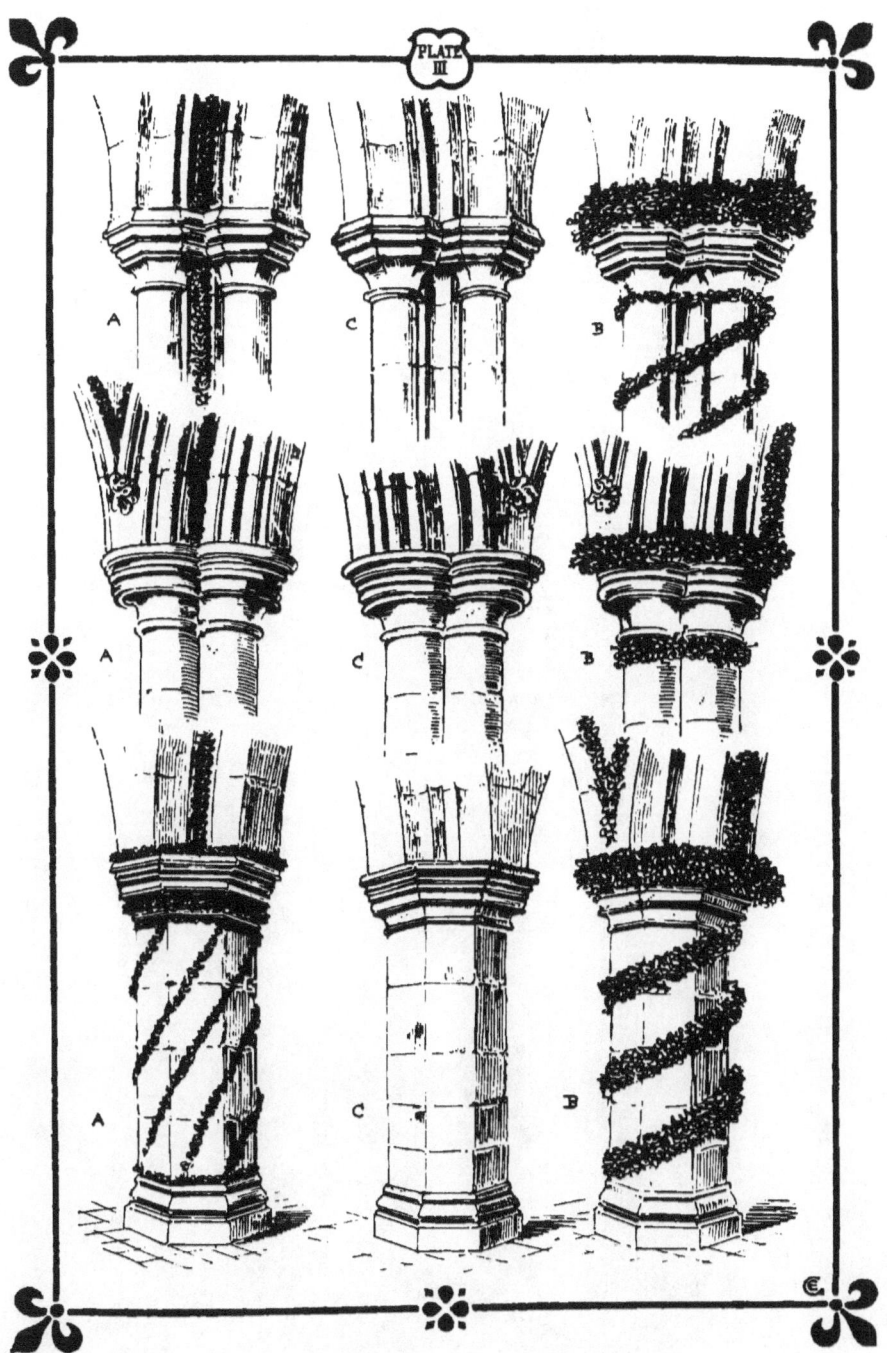

suitably be cusped, or traceried, or enriched, provided always that by nothing the style of the architecture is violated.

The figure here drawn is, perhaps, sufficient as a terrible example of false features. It also is a bad example of the breach of the following rule.

VI.

AVOID SAMENESS AND REPETITION.

As far as possible let there be no feeble repetition. If the hoops or wire frames used at one festival are again employed, try to vary their *position* as well as their vegetable or other covering.

Who does not know the weary anticipation which awaits the reappearance of a well-known interlaced triangle or vesica, or S. Andrew Cross, covered with blue flannel at Christmas, white at Easter, and red at Pentecost; or of a dingy "Ter-Sanctus," recurring with unfailing regularity upon the altar or screen? A little ingenuity, a little extra thought would prevent such distasteful monotony.

Above all, avoid meaningless multiplication of *symbols* and emblems.

If a Church is dedicated to S. Peter, do not let the cross-keys meet the eye at every turn; if to S. Andrew, let the X be varied by *something* else. There are few saints but have two or more emblems.*

So with the cross of CHRIST, the most sacred, yet, at the same time, the most vulgar of ornaments. Far too often it is used simply as a *dernier ressort* when invention fails. "Oh, put a cross," is an easy solution of a difficulty; but it is not reverent nor is it edifying, to see the symbol of redemption scattered broadcast. Specially should this be borne in mind on the Altar. If there is one cross upon the ledge no other is needed.

VII.

AVOID EXTRAVAGANCE.

Never try to beat the record. There is every reason for honestly and humbly trying to do better and better at every fresh attempt; but pray don't let it be

* See the list of emblems given in Chap. XIX.

your ambition that prompts you to "beat" anything you have ever done, and above all, don't try to beat your neighbour's efforts.

VIII.

Avoid Lack of Proportion.

"The better the day, the better the deed." Study the dignity of the Festival. Never let Christmas be overshadowed by a local Feast, or Easter and Whitsunday rank, as they so often do, below the level of the "Harvest Festival."

So look at the Calendar rather than your garden and conservatory. Don't fill your Church with roses simply because you have a plethora, or when "your chrysanthemums are a perfect dream," don't suppose that to be a sufficient reason for a dozen vases upon an altar that generally has but four!

Again, do not let the less sacred be more ornate than the more holy. Let the Porch lead to the Nave, the Nave to the Chancel, and that to the Sanctuary or the Eastern End. So with regard to the architecture, small aisles or transepts should not distract attention from the central line of the building.

So, too, with regard to the designs used. One should not by its discord or strong colouring throw another into the shade. There should be, in a word, unity of plan and harmony of detail. As Ruskin, in his *Seven Lamps of Architecture*, observes: "Our building, if it is well composed, is one thing, and is to be coloured as Nature would colour one thing—a shell, a flower, or an animal; not as she colours groups of things."

IX.

Avoid Unnecessary Offence.

Nothing should ever be done in the way of decoration that is likely to rouse even the stupidest opposition, or hurt the most senseless prejudice, without good reason. It is manifestly beyond human ingenuity to forecast the wonderful and unexpected avenues through which "offences may come."

The Churchwarden who read the sacred monogram as Pius X. will stand as a fair example of the type of mind with which we have sometimes to deal. But if we *know* for a certainty that half-a-dozen honest souls will be troubled by some misconstrued emblem or text, which has no necessary bearing upon the Festival, both we and they shall keep it in greater charity if we find something else.

X.

Reverence the Sanctuary.

Never do more work than is necessary *in the Church*, and *à fortiori* in the chancel. Avoid, so far as possible, making the sanctuary a workshop or a lumber-room.

If in the *unconsecrated* Temple, during its building, "no sound of axe or hammer" was heard, we may well think it unseemly that the sound of tools, the chatter of busy workers, and sometimes, alas! the wrangling of disputant decorators, should be heard in the chancel of a Christian Temple. Therefore, all larger work necessitating hammering, and entailing litter and rubbish, should be done in the school, the vicarage, or the nearest house; and each article, as it is finished, brought into the Church for fixture. Or else, if there is *no* convenient place near at hand, let the vestry be used in preference to the nave, the nave or aisles in preference to the chancel. Let all the workers honestly try to minimize the evil.

Without suggesting in this over-guilded age, the formation of yet another society, might we not well agree that just a word or two of prayer should always *precede* our work in Church?

Some such short devotion as this might serve :—

☩

In the Name of the Father . . .

℣. This is none other than the House of God;
℟. And this is the gate of heaven.
℣. The Lord loveth the gates of Zion;
℟. More than all the dwellings of Jacob.

Lord, have mercy . . .
Christ, have mercy . . .
Lord, have mercy . . .

Our Father . . .

℣. And lead us not into temptation;
℟. But deliver us from evil. Amen.

Collect.

Prevent us, O Lord . . .
The grace of our Lord . . .

☩

XI.

BE BUSINESS-LIKE.

A great deal of time would be saved if a meeting of those concerned were always summoned at the vicarage, or elsewhere, a week or so before each festival; so that a scheme or plan of campaign should be arranged before beginning the actual work. The division of labour, whereby the font is surrendered to one, and the pulpit to another, has its advantages, but its drawbacks also. Have we not often heard: "Miss Edwards' usual font," and "Miss Jones' everlasting lectern frill," spoken as cheap perennial jokes, pointed enough to sting, and true enough to show the danger of the allotment plan?

For these difficulties of working, the writer has no infallible remedy of his own to offer, but from the Book of Divine Wisdom he will venture to end his general principles with two all applicable maxims:—

(*a*) "Look not every one on *his own*, but on the things of others."

(*b*) "Let all your works be done with

CHARITY."

✠

CHAPTER III.

Of Wreaths and Garlands, and other Devices.

WREATHS have always formed, and should form, the staple garniture of any Church. They are both best and fittest, according to the Baconian maxim with which this treatise began.

They are, in every sense of the word, *evergreen!* We are scarcely likely to tire of the garniture that has served for (it may be) 5,000 years and will serve as long again if the world endure.

As garlands and wreaths will be required, a few hints should be given as to their arrangement, and the way of making them.

Suppose we deal first with the good old-fashioned wreath of evergreens. For its manufacture, we need a plentiful supply of small sprigs, such as would result from an ordinary use of the gardener's shears in trimming a holly or laurel hedge. Avoid the hacking and maiming of trees or bushes, and the useless littering of the scene of action that is inevitable, if you have large branches with "wood" in them. You will collect, then, a good store of holly and box, laurel, and so forth. Of these, by established precedence, holly takes the lead for Christmas, and is probably *never* used for any other decorations. But, as there are many odds and ends, the presence or absence of which may often lose a worker hours of precious time, there is here given a fairly exhaustive list of things required:

(*a*) Of purely vegetable matter to be wrought into the wreaths, and (*b*) the implements and accessories for the work.

(*a*) EVERGREENS, ETC.

Holly.	Ferns.
Variegated holly.	Fresh flowers and berries.
Ivy (the smaller kinds).	Privet.
Laurel.	Myrtle.
Box.	Euonymus.
Yew.	Cypress.
Everlasting flowers.	Cedar.
Fir (in its several varieties).	Bay.
Arbor vitæ.	Rosemary.
Portugal Laurel.	Moss.
Arbutus.	Grasses and rushes.
Laurestinus.	

With the above-named there ought to be sufficient variety for the satisfaction of most decorators' appetites; and, if the subjoined list be carefully attended to, the work can be begun.

(*b*) OTHER MATERIALS FOR FORMING WREATHS.

Rope.	Hoop iron.
Stout string.	Deal laths.
Fine twine.	Pocket knife.
Broad tape or carpet binding.	Two-foot rule.
Stout iron or copper wire.	Measuring-tape.
Fine „ „ „	Pencils and paper.
Reel-wire (as used by artificial flower-makers).	Pliers (for wire).
	Hammer.
Needles and thread.	Nails and tacks.
Scissors (best tied by a long tape to wrist or waist when in use).	Bands of perforated zinc.
	Zinc and iron clips for capitals of columns.

There are two or three different (or indifferent) ways of working a wreath, any of which may be employed.

The common method, and a good one, is to fasten the greenery with twine to a thin rope. How thick this should be depends on length, and so on, but for ordinary buildings a stout clothes line is, perhaps, a fair sample. The rope should be stretched, about three feet from the ground, across the room in which the decorators are working: if possible the *whole length* of each wreath should be in one stretch. Raised at this height from the floor it will be found easy to sit to one's work, and on either side and at intervals, there should be placed heaps, or baskets, of the evergreens to be used: *assorted*, if of various kinds, and clearly distinguishable. Small bunches of holly-berries, or everlastings, or other flowers to be "worked in," should be on a table close at hand.

The beginning is made (need I say it) at *one* end. A few sprigs are placed round the rope and tied to it firmly with fine twine, arranged so that neither it nor the stalks show over much. The next bunch will entirely hide the stalks of the first bunch when it is tied to the rope, and so on to the end. Nothing is simpler, and yet how often a wreath resembles a badly-packed carpet-bag, bulging in some places, and skimped in others. Only care is needed, but much of it.

The cautions may be briefly summarised thus:

(*a*) Be sure you put the same bulk on each time you advance a step; (*b*) Be sure you tie *each* bunch firmly; (*c*) Be sure that each step is the same *length;* that is to say, each tie should take place three, four, or five inches from the next.

There is a certain risk when using string, that it will slip loose upon the rope. I don't think it will do so if strongly and carefully tied, but at least it is safer to use thin wire of copper or iron instead of string: but never try to work a wreath without a continuous foundation. Often it comes to pass that a wreath simply looped together with string or wire, when it is hung up, unravels like this, to the loss of time and temper.

A wreath need not always be round, and, in fact, is often needed flat; for this purpose it will be found that rope, however thin, must be abandoned in favour of something thinner. Stout string or twine should be stretched, as already described, and on to this the sprigs of evergreen should be tied (with somewhat longer stalks) with their points directed *outwards*, instead of *along* the line of cord. They should however, always be fastened with *wire*, and not string.

The wreath itself may be broad or narrow, thick or slender, according to the position it has to occupy. The massive pillars of a Norman arcade will naturally demand a bolder treatment than a tiny shaft.

Some decorators prefer a stout wire as a foundation, and it has one evident advantage from its greater rigidity; which is, that it can be handled without *stretching*. The worker can sit in a chair, surrounded by the various materials, with the wire on his left hand. Taking the end of this over the knees, and unwinding it as required, the sprigs are then tied on with fine brass wire, and the finished wreath is paid out to the right hand, and laid upon a bench or table in large coils. The chief advantage of this mode of work is, perhaps, the fact that there is *no* limit of length except that of the hank or reel of wire; 100 feet can be made as simply as a yard.

Again, another excellent way is to use a flat foundation for a flat wreath. Broad worsted braid, or binding, or even narrow webbing, may be covered with evergreens by sewing them on with a needle and stout thread. To do this, it is as well to work at a table, with the braid tacked down in long lengths, or heavily weighted at either end, leaving sufficient play to raise the material when using the needle.

Another good foundation is wire ribbon, which can be treated just in the same manner, when the wreaths are to be hung or twined round columns; but supposing that they are to be used as "crowns" to encircle the capital of a shaft, or other convex surface, which does not give equal support at all points, and which yet demands a symmetrical and even curve, it is better to get some perforated zinc cut to the required size and shape, or a thin band of hoop iron, with holes punched at either end, which can be tied together with wire or string. Or when the work in hand is for lining out the inner curves and hollows of an arch, or a circular sinking, a *thin* lath of wood should be used, slightly notched along its edges, to give hold to the wire or string with which the evergreens are fastened. Such a lath, if rightly measured, will spring into its place and fix itself, without the slightest fear of its slipping, but it goes without saying that it *must* fit.

Plate III. shows the sort of "wreathage" recommended, and a study of the diagrams will convey a clearer impression than verbal description in each case. *C* shows the supposed portion of the Church to be wreathed, *B* the wrong way, and *A* the right way of treating it; not the *only* right way, but at least the most natural one.

Plate IV. also shows various "fillings-in" of blank spaces after the manner of diapers. These suppose, of course, that there is nothing better in existence—no panels or curtains, or any carved work to be hidden and disfigured.

A thin trellis-work of laths, covered with evergreens and flowers, would be the foundation, on which the ingenuity of the decorator can superimpose a great and wide variety of patterns. I see no objection to "backing" these frames with cloth or flannel or coloured *linen*, all of which materials can be got in excellent shades, and the prices are not exorbitant. Gilt or flock paper, glazed calico, and so forth, should be absolutely rejected as unworthy of employment.

In fixing all wreaths and other decorations, it is of the first importance to avoid the use of nails and tacks wherever possible; where they seem permissible they should be put with the greatest care. The havoc and destruction wrought by "hammer, saw, and plane" in our Churches is incalculable. Often one has sorrowfully to wait a twelvemonth before painting a wall, because the plaster is so broken and injured by "decorators" that it has to be patched and left to dry. Still oftener the wounded walls are left, with their gaping cracks and holes, abiding witnesses to the recklessness of careless hands.

One exception to the rule which forbids the use of nails on wood (see p. 10) may fairly be made in the case of large, rough beams, rafters, and wall plates.

Often in a village Church there are beams, perfectly plain and unwrought, crossing the nave or chancel at the plate level. Here it is quite permissible to drive in (and *leave*) at A. A. A. strong nails at regular intervals, for the suspension of wreaths and garlands.

So, too, at the cornice line nails or hooks or staples can be fixed without doing any damage. The double wire staples used by bell-hangers can be put without doing any damage, and are strong enough to carry a fair weight. A flexible wreath, when hung from two points,

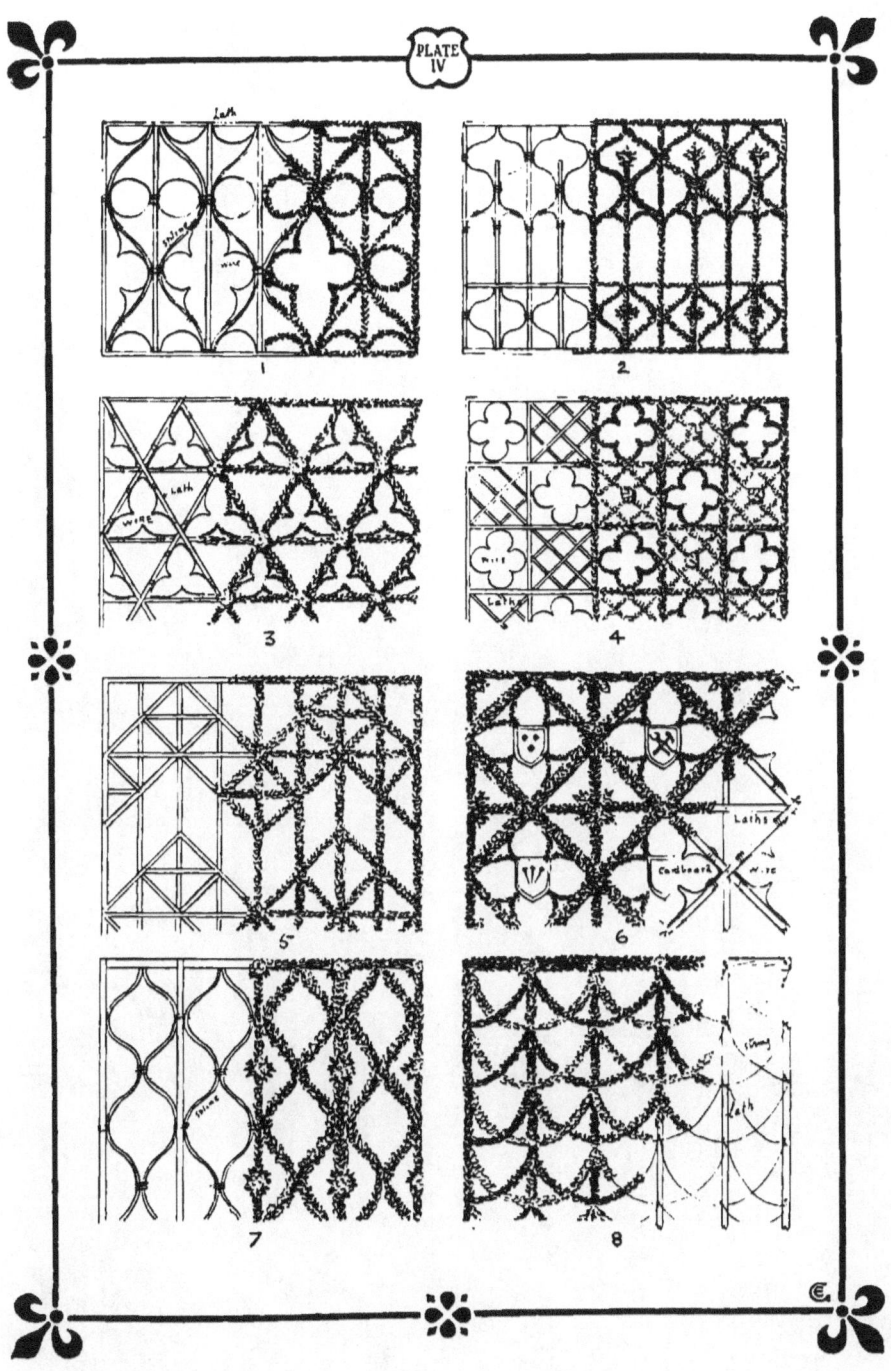

assumes by its own weight a curve which no art of man could better. The *catenary* of the suspension bridge, or even the slack clothes-line or telegraph-wire give examples of this beautiful line, and it is capable of infinite variation. The droop may be slight, so that the curve is very gentle (1), or sharp and deeper (as in 2 and 3); so that its depth may equal or exceed its width.

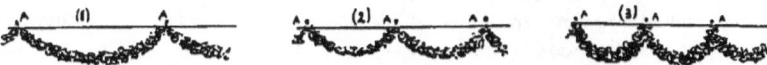

One caution is not superfluous : take the greatest care that all the curves are *equal*, whatever their form, or the wreath will look untidy and restless.

Another form of festoon is that of a double, intersecting wreath (4). If made with two garlands of different tints, the effect of the interlaced wreaths is very happy. Say that you take one of pale holly or golden euonymus and another of dark yew or box, or in any other way counterchange the colours, you will certainly get a good return for your trouble.

When such decorations are only needed for a day, and where there is no fear of neglect, your garlands may be brightened with flowers—peonies or chrysanthemums, daffodils and daisies. But, alas, experience has shown too often that zeal cools and flowers fade, when the feast has come and gone. Moreover, it is difficult and not always seemly, to have to drag in ladders and all the *impedimenta* of garnishing, so as to mount to beam and cornice for the removal of flowers. Our neighbours across the channel have solved the difficulty by using paper roses and dyed moss for their May-garlands, suspended throughout the month of May, but we cannot say "they manage these things better in France."

There is a use of evergreens of a far less artificial sort than that mentioned hitherto, *i.e.*, the use of whole *branches* of evergreens and the hanging from the walls or roof long runners of ivy. This sometimes looks well, and so does another plan, when one can steadfastly shut the eyes of one's memory and refuse to see the Noah's-ark trees of childhood—I mean the placing of bushes and fir trees in tubs and ranking them down the aisles; the latter plan, however, leaves little room for worshippers, if the trees are large, and none for the decorator.

Of Devices (other than Wreaths).

Here it is to be feared the readers will experience a want of sympathy, and be inclined to complain, with a reader of a former publication of mine, "The writer seems to object to *all* decorations!"

So soon as the spirit of enterprise stirred the hearts of those who used to deck our Churches for Christmastide, they began casting about for something more "emblematical" than a wreath on a beam or a branch of holly stuck on a pew end.

The tracery of the windows, or the carving of the benches, suggested trefoils, circles, and quatrefoils. The symbolism of Christianity easily provided them with crosses, and monograms, and stars; while the winter landscape unhappily lay open to the base imitation of cotton wool-snow and Epsom-frost.

Putting aside the latter monstrosities, let us ask what should be said about the first-named decorations?

A trefoil (or a circle, or what not) is an excellent form and a beautiful symbol; but *where* are you to put it? Our forerunners of the 60's or 70's drove a nail in wherever it would stick; and hung up a hoop or wooden frame, covered with holly, by a string on the wall, or in the stall front or elsewhere, and therewith were well content. They probably hung up a round dozen of *one* form in different parts of the building, and if they alternated the circles with crosses, they felt that the force of imagination would carry them no further.

But the study of symbolism and the impulse of emulation did carry people further before long; and devices grew and multiplied, until latterly many of our Churches have been perfect museums of ingenuity, affording a rich supply of copy to the correspondents of the county press.

"The walls of the sacred edifice were garnished with symbolic devices: the circle of eternity alternating with the impressive sign of the Trinity; while at intervals were numerous crosses and monograms, the work of the devoted ladies at the Rectory."

"The font was undertaken by the Misses Taylor, of Plucky Hall, whose deft fingers have unmistakably left their mark upon the sacred basin, and enriched its chaste outlines with appropriate and holy signs. . . ."

This is the sort of terrible nonsense we are all too familiar with, in the columns of the local news; but is the description much worse than the things described?

By the mere hanging up of circles and triangles here and there, the dabbing on to stalls and reading-desks of paper shields with gilt monograms, a Church is in no true sense of the word decorated. But do not let my readers suppose that there is no room for effort nor hope of success.

There is plenty of room for the placing of the trefoil, or the shield, or other device—if you can find it; such places being specially those which offer *containing lines*: a "blind" arch, a sunk panel (containing nothing), the space between a double lancet and the crown of the arch, the tympanum of a door, the spandrels of an arcade, and so on. In all these places your devices may fairly be hung or fitted.

On plate V. there are drawn a large number of "foundations" for such devices, which may be bordered with evergreens or everlasting flowers; and the centres

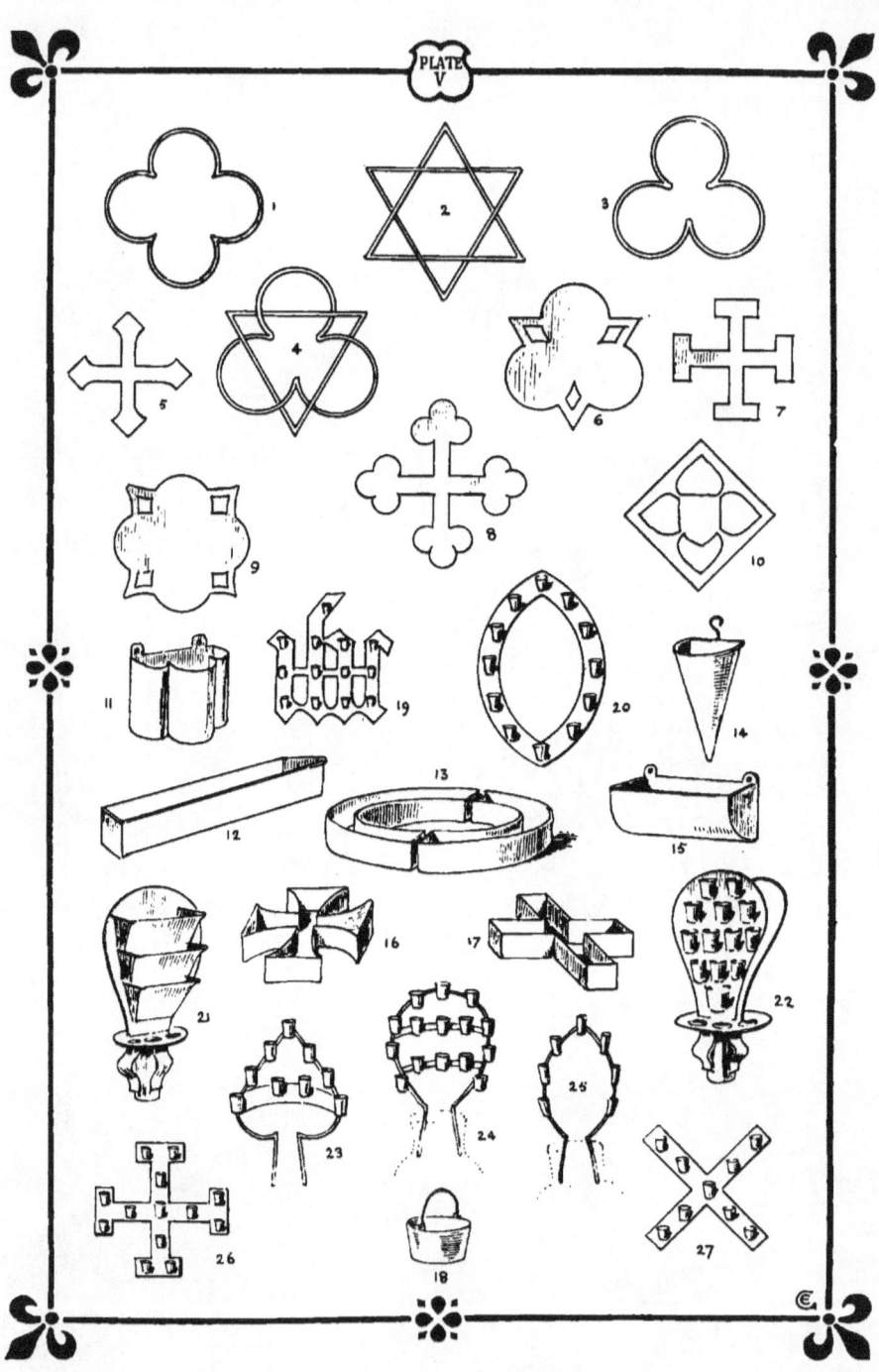

may be illuminated with colours, painted preferably in oil on canvas—*never* in cut-out coloured paper gummed together.

It may be that oil painting is beyond the power of some whose fingers are yet well able to colour in water medium. In this case good cartridge paper or slightly tinted cardboard can be used, and the emblems chosen can be painted on. The second part of the manual enters far more fully into the history and rationale of symbolism than may be thought necessary for the mere purposes of ordinary "decoration." Undoubtedly this is the case; but my readers will probably agree with me that it is better to give too much rather than too little in the way of information, and the aim of the book is to encourage further study, and not merely to save trouble, by finding an emblem "ready to hand." Nor is it intended to be used as a mere index. Though it does little more than touch the fringes of the vast domain of sacred archæology, it is, so far as it goes, a treatise and not a "catalogue." As to the use of symbolic shapes I think I will let the diagrams on Plate V. speak for themselves. It is impossible to lay down universally applicable rules, or even suggestions worthy of reliance. A few mistakes, rectified by experience, a few endeavours, and conscientious efforts will, in all likelihood, bring the reward of success.

Chapter II. has cleared the way, and marked out the path, so far, at least, as I can show it, and I must leave my readers (even if they consent to be disciples), somewhat of a free hand.

I must now give some description of the

IRONMONGERY

employed in such decoration as we are concerned with, and illustrated on Plate V.

The foundations for wreathage and emblems here shown may be of wood, or cane, or metal. Figs. 1, 2, 3, 4 show the most convenient way of having well-formed and rigid shape on which to work, made of strong galvanized wire. Figs. 5, 6, 7, 8, 9, 10 show forms cut out in zinc, either solid or perforated. Figs. 11, 12, 13, 14, 15, 16, 17, 18 represent the various contrivances for supplying water to fresh flowers. All of these can easily be made of tin or zinc, and should be strongly painted with three or four coats before use.

Each trough (like 12) should be *numbered* to its position in window-sill or base of screen, or what not; and all such vessels should be well rinsed out, and carefully dried when put away. Figs. 19, 20, 26, 27 show how hanging crosses, monograms, or geometrical forms can have the enrichment of living flowers without the otherwise inevitable decay. Figs. 21, 22, 23, 24, 25 are different forms of the "fans" used for displaying altar bouquets.

Exception may be taken to the employment of any such mechanical making up of a nosegay on the score of unreality; yet in large Churches it may be argued in defence, that without some such means cut flowers will be practically invisible. Granting this, we may probably feel free to use the most convenient method of display. The form assumed by the frame has become so stereotyped, that in

Spain, at least, the altar bouquets are cut out of a flat sheet of metal, chased and embossed sometimes in silver; sometimes out of the commonest tin plate, splashed with a few daubs of red and white and green.

As no one could ever dream of going further and faring worse, this will form an appropriate tailpiece to the chapter, since it is surely the decorators' *dernier ressort!*

CHAPTER IV.

Floral Decoration.

WHERE living flowers are used, arrangements must of course be made for the stalks to be kept moist; and this can very easily be done by water contained in little zinc tubes, which can be soldered in any position on to iron frames, or these zinc tubes (formed as cones, and made with a hook) can be hung on any part of the decorations required. A drop of thin gum in each of the flowers will prevent them falling to pieces as soon as they otherwise would. The stalks can be dipped in hot sealing-wax. For altar-vases, useful frames are made in zinc, which enable the decorator to make an effective bouquet with a small supply of flowers; that is to say, provided it is thought well to have the large upstanding bouquets of symmetrical form that seem so generally demanded. I am not sure that smaller and less formal "posies" do not look better, but that is a matter of taste.

Large flower-pots or jardinières, filled with growing plants, azaleas, camellias, heath, and so on, may advantageously be put in front of the screen, in large window-sills, or flanking the altar. But let us avoid the terrible excesses of the typical West End wedding, whereby the sanctuary is perverted to a horticultural show; where indiarubber plants and cabbage palms wave their branches for awhile, till they are carted off to do duty at a political banquet or a Lord Mayor's Show.

Flowers on the altar, and around it, are beautiful and edifying; but hired exotics are a mere disfigurement, and a cumbering of the ground.

When arranging flowers upon the altar, take care that they are *safe*, *i.e.*, that there be no fear of their falling upon the *mensa*. Also see that they do not so stand in front of the altar-lights as by their shadows to make it difficult for the celebrant to *read*.

The use of flowers, although ancient and laudable, is not subject to any definite rules or laws. Fads and superstitions there are enough and to spare. I have before now been told my altar was bare, because there were no *white* flowers, and "only white must be used." Or some more generous decorator would allow white and red, but nothing else; or blue, if it is S. Mary's!

All this is sheer nonsense. "GOD made every tree to grow," and painted every flower. Whatsoever is beautiful and sweet may be used freely. There is only one rule which, perhaps, may be laid down, and that is: a purple frontal should mean *no flowers*. This rule, however, is commonly relaxed on three days: the Third Sunday in Advent, with its introit, *Gaudete*; the Fourth Sunday in Lent, *Lætare*; and the Holy Innocents' Day.

On Palm Sunday the "decorations" may, by ancient custom, include box, and yew, and willow, as well as the "real palms" with which the altar will probably be decked.

Of flowers at funerals, we may heartily sympathize with the frequent notices in the *Times*: "No flowers by request!"

In seeking to banish the skull and crossbones, and the grim ghastliness of the last century, we have run to the opposite extreme, and made the coffin a garish and ostentatious flower show, a vehicle too, alas! of unreal "sympathy" and "kindest regards," that cannot sufficiently be condemned.

By all means let a few simple flowers be strewn by the grave side, and let, perhaps, one cross or wreath be placed upon the pall; is not that enough?

Flowers should never be used in decoration unless they are in water, or are capable of constant renewal; otherwise an "octave" affords a dismal sight, and an unsavoury odour. At the base of the screen, round the font, and in the window-sills, troughs of zinc, painted a quiet colour, can always be put, if one will spend a few shillings for the sake of decency and cleanliness.

These troughs can either have a floating board pierced with holes, or a wire lid, or they can be filled with watered moss; or damp clay or sand will keep many flowers excellently—the primroses of our Easter octave, for instance.

Flowers, again, might well be more used than they are for the decoration of GOD'S acre. On anniversary or "year's mind," it were well if we remembered the sleeping-places of our own loved ones; and at Easter (and on All Souls' Day) it is surely fitting to deck the whole ground at once.

EVERLASTING FLOWERS, BERRIES, AND MOSS

may all be used for making wreaths, or "devices" to hang upon the walls or other suitable parts of the Church.

For working with the everlasting flowers most people prefer a groundwork of perforated zinc, cut out to the required shape, as the stalks can be put through the holes and fastened behind either with cotton, or by pasting or glueing stout brown paper over the back. Another plan is to have the groundwork shaped out of cardboard or of a thin piece of wood, which should be either covered with paper or painted, and on this the flowers, cut from the stalks, are fastened down either with glue, very thick gum, or shoemakers' paste.

Melted gelatine will be found more useful than gum arabic for fixing the flowers and berries. The gelatine can be spread over the device, and the flowers laid on; but for berries it is best to dip them in a saucer containing the gelatine.

Supposing either of the above plans to be adopted, the worker should procure the device selected, cut out to the required size, and then lay it down on a piece of plain paper, and with a pencil trace the shape. Then remove the zinc, and with water-colours try the effect of the various shades it is proposed to use; for it should always be borne in mind that it is *not* requisite to adhere to one colour only with these decorations. Thus, a star, instead of being all yellow, may have

the principal part yellow, with a green centre, and a line of red around the outside edge. A double triangle may have one yellow, edged with red, and the other white, edged with blue.

By trying the effect on paper in the way suggested, one is much more likely to get a satisfactory result, and it will also save time in arranging the flowers.

There are many varieties of everlastings: the small *gnaphalium*, the larger *helichrysum*, and the white Cape everlasting. With these be content, and if you want colour brighter than the natural flowers provide, use holly berries or the brilliant hips and haws, or the berries of the nightshade, that are to be found in every hedgerow.

White Cape everlastings are very useful for decorations; but the seed in the centre should be removed, and they should be warmed by steam or in front of a fire, opened out flat, and turned face downwards, leaving the back uppermost. When so used, a comparatively small number are required. They are also used the other way, much closer together. The Cape silver leaves are very effective, and there are also many very beautiful *grasses*, too often disfigured by being dyed bright blue or red, but easily to be obtained *au naturel;* these are useful and legitimate substitutes for flowers in the winter season, and may even be placed in vases on the altar without incongruity.

DEVICES IN EVERGREENS.

For forming devices, either entirely of evergreens, or of evergreens with the addition of a few everlasting flowers, perforated zinc is, perhaps, the best groundwork. The plan to be adopted for fixing them is as follows:—First procure the materials required, viz., the forms it is proposed to decorate, a supply of evergreen leaves, and very small sprays of evergreens, some stout needles, and strong thread of a dark colour—that used for sewing carpets, or ordinary black thread will do.

(1)

(2)

Commence sewing on the leaves and sprays at the bottom of the device, taking care that the thread fastens the leaves down across one of the veins, and that the stalks are as far as possible covered by other leaves. For devices that are intended to be fixed at a slight elevation, small leaves should be used, and the work should be done as neatly as possible; but for those that are to be fixed at a considerable height, larger

(3)

(4)

(5)

leaves will be more effective. Devices consisting entirely of evergreens have a somewhat heavy appearance. This is relieved by small bunches of holly berries, or flowers introduced in different parts of the design, in the way indicated by figs. 1, 2, 3, 4, 5.

As popular belief has always associated particular flowers with certain saints, it is quite possible that the list here appended is more or less dependable. As the daisy is S. Margaret's flower, and the white lily has ever been called the "lady lily," so S. John gives the name to the beautiful yellow wort, and so in many other cases. At the same time, one cannot read the names of many of these "appropriated" flowers without a sceptical feeling of something more than doubt with regard to their antiquity. The *chrysanthemum*, for instance, for S. Simon has a somewhat modern flavour! and the *ricinus* for Palm Sunday provokes a sense of nausea. "Palmchrist" is simply the *castor oil plant*.

However, failing the requisite knowledge of sacred botany, I append this list "for what it is worth," taken bodily from a book by W. A. Barrett, entitled, *Flowers and Festivals*:—

JANUARY.

1 The Circumcision. Laurestinus, *Viburnum tinus*.
6 The Epiphany. Common Star of Bethlehem, *Ornithogalum umbellatum*.
8 S. Lucian, P.M. Common laurel, *Laurus*.
13 S. Hilary, B.C.D. Barren strawberry, *Fragaria sterilis*.
18 S. Prisca, V.M. Four-toothed moss, *Brynm pellucidum*.
20 S. Fabian, B.M. Large dead nettle, *Lamium garganicum*.
21 S. Agnes, V.M. Black hellebore or Christmas rose, *Helleborus niger, Flore albo*.
22 S. Vincent, D.M. Early willow grass, *Draba verna*.
25 Conversion of S. Paul. Winter hellebore, *Helleborus hyemalis*.

FEBRUARY.

2 Purification of B.V.M. Snowdrops, *Galanthus nivalis*.
3 S. Blasius, B.M. Great water moss, *Fontinalis antipyretica*.
5 S. Agatha, V.M. Common primrose, *Primula vulgaris*.
14 S. Valentine, B.M. Yellow crocus, *Crocus aureus*.
24 S. Matthias. Mezereon, *Daphne Mezereum*.

MARCH.

1 S. David, Abp. C. Leek, *Allium porrum*.
2 S. Chad, B.C. Dwarf chickweed, *Cerastium pennilum*.
7 S. Perpetua, M. Early daffodil, *Narcissus pseudo Narcissus simplex*.
12 S. Gregory, B.C.D. Channelled ixia, *Ixia bulbocodium*.
17 S. Patrick, B.C. Shamrock, trefoil, *Trifolium repens*.
18 S. Edward, K.M. Great leopard bane, *Doronicum pardalianches*.
21 S. Benedict, Ab. Herb bennet, *Geum urbanum*; and way bennet or wild rye, *Hordeum murinum*; also, bulbous fumitory, *Fumaria bulbosa*.
25 The Annunciation. Marigold, *Calendula officinalis*.

APRIL.

3 S. Richard, B.C. Evergreen alkanet, *Anchusa sempervireus.*
4 S. Ambrose, B.C.D. Meadow orchis, *Orchis mascula.*
19 S. Alphege, Abp. M. Ursine garlic, *Allium ursinum.*
23 S. George, M. Harebell, *Hyacinthus nonscriptus.*
25 S. Mark, E. Clarimond tulip, *Tulipa præcox.*

MAY.

1 S. Philip, A.M. Red tulip, *Tulipa Gesueri.*
3 Invention of the Cross. White narcissus, *Narcissus poeticus.*
19 S. Dunstan, Abp. C. Monkshood, *Aconitum Napellus.*
26 S. Augustine, Abp.C. Rhododendron, *Rhododendron ponticum.*
27 Ven. Bede, P.C. Yellow bachelor's button, *Ranunculus acris.*

JUNE.

1 S. Nicomede, P.M. Single yellow rose, *Rosa lutea.*
5 S. Boniface, B.M. Three-leaved rose, *Rosa sinica.*
11 S. Barnabas, A.M. Midsummer daisy, *Chrysanthemum leucanthemum.*
17 S. Alban, M. Feather grass, *Stipa pennata.*
24 Nativity of S. John Baptist. S. John's wort, *Hypericum pulchrum.* Tutsam, *Hypericum Androsæmum.* Chrysanthemum, also gooseberries.
29 S. Peter, A.M. Yellow rattle, *Rhinanthus Christa-galli.*

JULY.

2 Visitation of B.V.M. White lily, *Lilium candidum.*
15 S. Swithun, B.C. Small cape marigold, *Calendula pluvialis.*
20 S. Margaret, V M. Virginia dragon's-head, *Dracocephalum virginianum.*
22 S. Mary Magdalene. African lily, *Agapanthus umbellatus.*
25 S. James, A.M. S. James' Cross, *Amaryllis formosissima.* S. James' wort, *Senecio Jacobæa.*
26 S. Anne. Common chamomile, *Anthemis nobilis.*

AUGUST.

1 Lammas Day, *i.e.,* "S. Peter ad Vincula." Stramony, *Datura stramonium.*
6 Transfiguration. Common meadow saffron, *Colchicum autumnale.*
7 Holy Name of JESUS. Common amaranth, *Amaranthus hypochondriacus.*
10 S. Laurence, D.M. Common balsam, *Impatiens balsamina.*
15 Assumption of B.V.M. Virgin's bower, *Clematis vitalba.*
24 S. Bartholomew, A.M. Sunflower, *Helianthus annuus.*
28 S. Augustine, B.C.D. Golden rod, *Solidago virgnrea.*
29 Beheading of S. John Baptist. S. John's wort, *Hypericum Elodes.*

SEPTEMBER.

1 S. Giles, Ab. S. Giles' orpine, *Sedum telephium.*
7 S. Enurchus, B.C. Starwort, *Callitriche autumnualis.*
8 Nativity of B.V.M. Bryony, our Lady's Seal. Red berried bryony, *Bryonia dioica.*
14 Holy Cross Day. Blue passion flower, *Passiflora cærulea.*
17 S. Lambert, B.M. Narrow-leaved mallow, *Malva augustifolia.*
21 S. Matthew, A.M. Ciliated passion flower, *Passiflora ciliata.*
26 S. Cyprian, Abp. M. Starwort, *Aster tripolium.*
29 S. Michael and All Angels. Michaelmas daisy, *Aster Tradescauti.*
30 S. Jerome, P.C.D. Golden amaryllis, *Amaryllis aurea.*

OCTOBER.

1 S. Remigius, Abp. C. Lowly amaryllis or S. Remy's lily, *Amaryllis humilis.*
6 S. Faith, V.M. Late feverfew, *Pyrethrum serotinum.*
9 S. Denys, B.M. Milky Agaric, *Agaricus lactiflorus.*
17 S. Etheldreda, Q.V.C. Ten-leaved sunflower, *Helianthus decapetalus.*
18 S. Luke, E. Floccose agaric, *Agaricus floccosus.*
25 S. Crispin, M. Flea-bane starwort, *Aster conizoides.*
28 SS. Simon and Jude, AA.MM. S. Simon, late chrysanthemum, *Chrysanthemum serotinum.* S. Jude, scattered starwort, *Aster passiflorus.*

NOVEMBER.

1 All Saints. Sweet bay, *Laurus nobilis.* Dark red sunflower, *Helianthus atro-rubens.*
6 S. Leonard, D.C. Yew, *Taxus baccata.*
11 S. Martin, B.C. Weymouth pine, *Pinus strobus.*
13 S. Britius or Brice, B.C. Bay, *Laurus poeticus.*
15 S. Machutus, B.C. Sweet coltsfoot, *Tussilago fragrans.*
17 S. Hugh, B.C. Tree stramony, *Datura arborea.*
20 S. Edmund, K.M. Red stapelia, *Stapelia rufa.*
22 S. Cecilia, V.M. Trumpet-flowered wood sorrel, *Orchis tubiflora.*
23 S. Clement, B.M. Convex wood sorrel, *Oxalis convexula.*
25 S. Catharine, V.M. Sweet butter bur, *Petasites vulgaris.*
30 S. Andrew. S. Andrew's cross, *Ascyrus vulgaris.*

DECEMBER.

6 S. Nicholas, B.C. Nest-flowered heath, *Erica nidiflora.*
8 Conception of B.V.M. Abor vitæ, *Thuja occidentalis.*
13 S. Lucy, V.M. Cypress abor vitæ, *Thuja cupresoides.*
21 S. Thomas, A.M. Sparrow wort, *Erica passerina.*
25 Christmas Day. Holly, *Ilex bacciflora.*
26 S. Stephen, D.M. Purple Heath, *Erica purpurea.*
27 S. John, A.E. Flame heath, *Erica flamma.*
28 Holy Innocents or Childermas. Bloody heath, *Erica cruenta.*
31 S. Sylvester, B.C. Genista heath, *Erica genistopha.*

MOVEABLE FEASTS.

Passion Sunday. Christ's thorn, *Paliurus aculeatus*.
Palm Sunday. Common palma Christi, *Ricinus communis*.
Maundy Thursday. Laurel-leaved passion flower, *Passiflora rubra*.
Good Friday. Long-sheathed anemone, *Anemone pulsatilla*; also called passion flower.
Easter Eve. Spear-leaved violet, *Viola lactea*.
Easter Day. White lily, *Lilium candidum*.
Rogation Sunday. Rogation flower, *Polygala vulgaris*. Common milk-wort.
Ascension Day. Lilies of the valley, *Convallaria majalis*.
Whitsun Day. Columbine, *Aquilegia vulgaris*. White thorn, *Prunus spinosa*.
Trinity Sunday. Herb Trinity, *Viola tricolor*, also called pansy; violet, heart's-ease, common white trefoil, *Trifolium repens*.

Of Lights used decoratively.

As in the chamber used for S. Paul's farewell Eucharist at Troas, often there are many lights burning in our Churches, but seldom, I think, are they used, as they might be, for purely decorative purposes.

True, there are (for evening services) enough gas jets or electric bulbs for all practical use, and on the altar there are frequently to be seen multitudes of little branched candlesticks, so that the twin lights "for the signification of the Light of the World" are multiplied indefinitely.

But neither the utilitarian provision for reading hymn-books, nor the festal use of many tapers crowded together on the altar, quite constitute the "decorative" use of lights, by which I mean their use in *conjunction* with floral and evergreen garnishing.

It will probably be objected: "How like a Christmas-tree!" Yes; but it is doubtful whether any object is *more* festal, more utterly joyous than this friend of our childhood. I do not advocate the introduction of the thing itself, but only the use of the same combination of bright light and dark colour.

If a large beam is wreathed, and hung with evergreens, why not surmount it with large standing tapers? These may be placed either on mere spikes, or in simple stands of wrought iron, like F; or even in more elaborate candlesticks of turned brass, like G. The old-fashioned sconces and prickets may well be used upon the walls. These, too, can be either the roughest structures of lath and wire, covered with box or yew, like D or E. Or they may be of wrought metal, ornamented to any pitch of beauty. The accompanying sketches—A, B, and C—are simply given as suggestions.

If the simple forms are used, the village blacksmith and the ironmonger can supply all that is needed. The actual sockets in which the candles are fixed should be made of tin or iron, and *always* of a curved or "saucer" shape, otherwise, if the candles flare and gutter in the wind, the results may be disastrous to the clothing of the worshippers below.

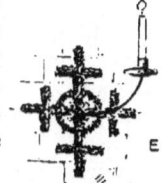

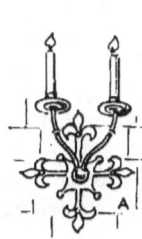
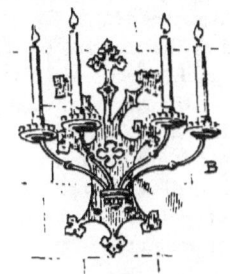
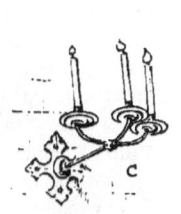

The figure (1) shows the shape of socket sufficiently clearly; these may serve for fastening, either to the branched candlestands, as on fig. 4, or they may be grouped into a corona, as in fig. 3.

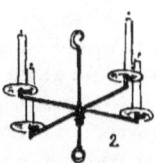
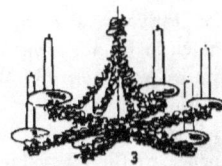
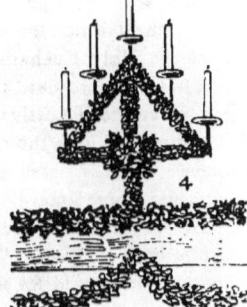

I have not thought it worth while to draw any more elaborate *corona lucis* than one of simple iron, capable of local manufacture, though it goes without saying that, when funds allow, nothing gives greater lustre and brightness to a Church than hanging lights in frames of brass or copper, or gilded iron-work.

CHAPTER V.

Of Colours.

WHETHER we are concerned with the flowers, the decorations, the vestments, or ornaments of the Church, the colours employed have without doubt *some* significance.

So far as the liturgical colours are concerned, according to the prevailing Western use, the meaning of them is fairly set forth, thus:

WHITE signifies innocence, glory, and joy.

RED, the fire of love which the HOLY GHOST kindles and sheds forth within us; or again the blood of the martyrs, the fairest flowers of love.

GREEN, the hope and desire of heaven; and also the life of Christians, which, planted by the word of GOD, grow and flourish in the light of His example. Our LORD indeed compares Himself to a green tree, saying, "If they shall do these things in a green tree;" and of the righteous it is written, "they shall flourish as a green tree," "and their leaf shall not wither."

PURPLE, which is a sort of mean between red and black, denotes penitence, fasting, and the like, by which, through the Blood of CHRIST, we escape the death of sin and hell.

BLACK is the sign of death and darkness, by which we are reminded of the souls of the faithful, for whom we can plead the everlasting light, in the Sacrifice of the Holy Eucharist.

These colours date from the twelfth century, before which time vestments seem to have been mostly white. The Eastern Church knows no definite "sequence" of colours, but uses the most beautiful of any colour on high days, preferring, however, white if possible for festivals. A comparative table of colours, shewing Sarum use where known, is given in Blunt's *Annotated Prayer Book*.

So far well and good, but we are often told that if we would be English we must go back to "Sarum" and unearth the sequence of the past. There would be something to be said for this, were it possible to discover the old use; but it is not. In spite, or rather in consequence, of the many books and articles written thereon, we are forced to the conclusion that we had better plead ignorance, and that the writers of the said books would have done well to plead the same.

On the one hand, we have been told that the Sarum use had *yellow* for confessors and *blue* for the Virgin, and infinite varieties of chequered and parti-coloured vestments.

But on the other, we are told with a certainty and finality worthy of the chair of S. Peter, that only white and red and blue were used. Other still more sure and certain guides prove absolutely that only white and red were ever worn by the true disciples of S. Osmund—white for Christmas and Lent and Easter; red for ordinary Sundays and for Advent! How these wonderful statements are to be reconciled with the far more weighty evidence of unnumbered inventories and countless pictures, I must leave to others to decide.

For the distribution of the colours among the days of the year my readers are referred to such kalendars as they may account the safest guides.

BLUE is said to be the colour of our Lady, also of heaven.

GOLD signifies glory, and one cannot quarrel with the fitness of it, but why yellow should be commonly called the colour of a "confessor," or why grey should be supposed to figure innocence falsely accused, as the Spaniards say, *quien sabe*.

A common feeling of the fitness of things suggests that, so far as the moveable drapery of the Church is concerned, all should be of a suit. This is often carried too far. There is no sequence of book markers, not even in the illustrious Church of Sarum.

Mats and carpets may be left alone, even though they differ from the frontal; it is certainly needless to stuff the communicants' kneeler into a long purple "sack" for Lent: though, of course, if the wealth of a parish allows, it is good and seemly to have hangings and tapestries of all sorts, suitable to various times and seasons.

With regard to colour, as applied to floral decoration, whether of the altar or the whole Church, clearly there is a fitness in the use of as much white as possible on white days, and of red at Pentecost, and of blue and white on feasts of the Virgin; but to say that blue is *unfit* for Easter, or red or yellow, or indeed *any* colour, is to go beyond all reason and sense.

The heraldic use of colours will be fully explained in Chapter XXI., on the "Heraldry of the Shield," which I would ask my readers to study attentively.

Of Forms and Figures.

There is a certain symbolism in the forms and figures taken by Church furniture and utensils, as also by more decorative objects. This may be seen from the fact that some shapes are universally employed, and others as absolutely prohibited. A triangular or circular altar, for instance, would be inadmissible.

An altar is always a cube, having the square measures of the cross: length, and breadth, and depth, and height.

A font has three shapes, and only three.* It is circular, because the baptism is for the round world and them that dwell therein; or it is octagonal, because of the eight persons who were saved by water from perishing; or it is square, by reason of the north and the south and east and west, whence the regenerate shall come to sit down with the children of Abraham in the Kingdom.

* To this rule, as to all others, there are a few rare exceptions: Pugin mentions Hollington Font as *five sided*, Bredon, Farringdon, Carlisle, and Ramsey as *six sided*, and Chaddesden as *seven sided*.

Briefly, the symbolism of figures may be stated thus:
The circle stands for the world, and for eternity;
The triangle, or trefoil,
The interlaced circles and } stand for the Blessed Trinity;
The interlaced triangles
The octagon typifies regeneration;
The square, or four-foil, indicates the cross (and the world ruled by the cross).
The five-fold form or figure, or the number five, the five wounds.

The seven-foil, or other grouping of seven, figures not only the perfect number, but the seven gifts of the HOLY GHOST, and the Seven Spirits of GOD before the throne in heaven.

The number two is said to figure the double nature of our Blessed LORD, but this can scarcely be said to be a matter of intention save in the rarest instances.

"All things are made double" by the Almighty, says the Wise Man, and natural balance demands the "setting of one against another."

Even the "two lights" upon the altar are, by no means of necessity, employed. "At least one" is the ancient requirement, and I have myself seen an altar in a Spanish Church with only one candle upon it.

There is ever a danger of over refinement and scrupulosity in using shapes deemed symbolical. This, however, applies perhaps rather to architecture than decoration. The post-reformation canon of the English Church which forbids a western triplet, for fear of dishonouring the Trinity, has, perhaps, done something towards fostering hyper-sensitiveness in this direction.

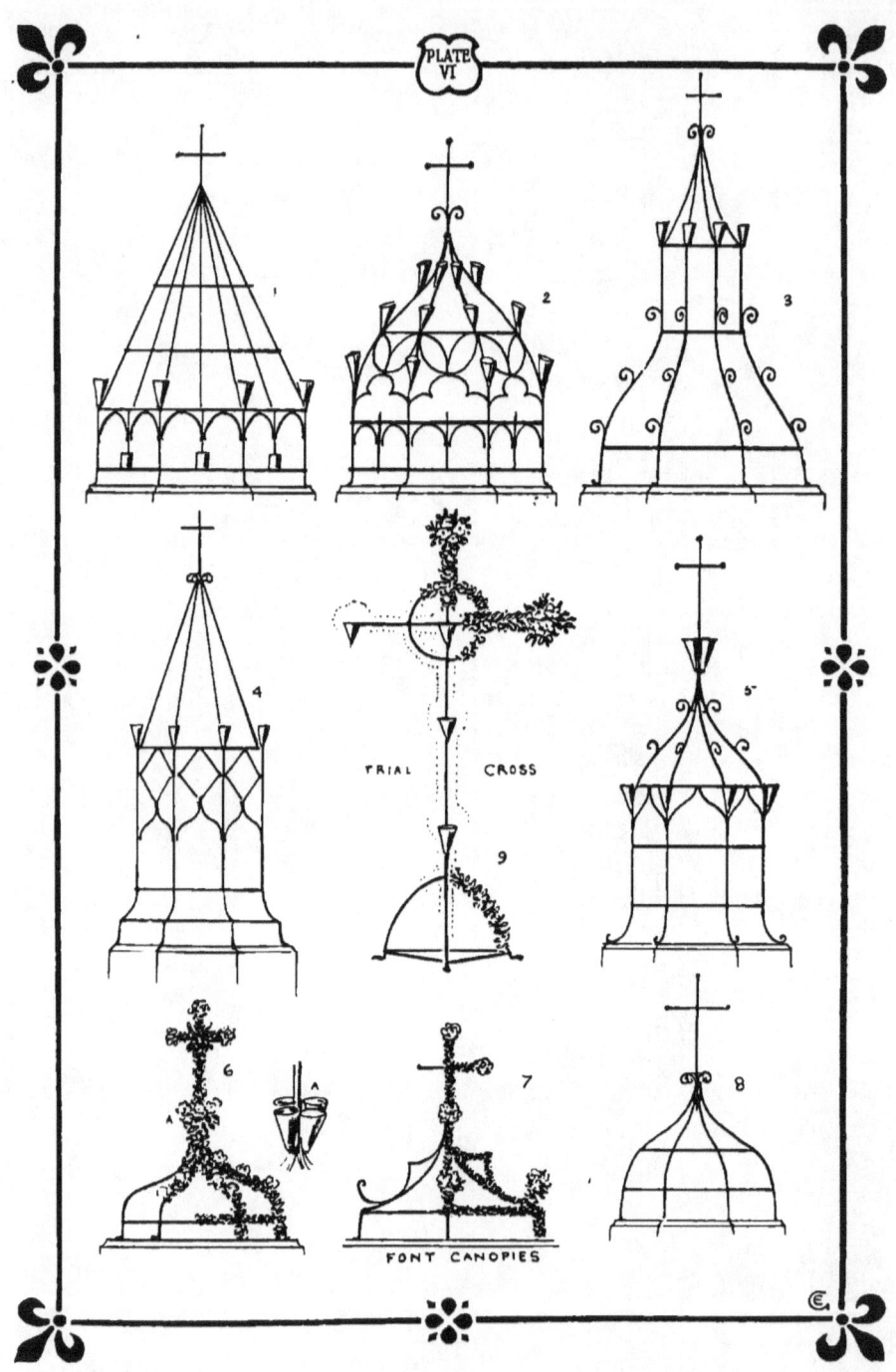

CHAPTER VI.

Of temporary structures.

UNDER this heading will stand (or fall) temporary screens, crosses, and font covers.

We will take the font cover first. Too often, unfortunately, the wire-work cover is regarded as a permanent utensil of the Church; and, being far "prettier" than a flat lid or plain oak canopy, we see the true cover rolled away behind the stove, or otherwise displaced, and a wire cage substituted. If *this* is intended, there is nothing more to be said about such a monstrosity; but if the wire frame is simply meant to show what a canopy could be—if it is clearly meant to be a step onwards and upwards—by all means take it and deck it to the best of your powers. On Plate VI. I have figured several of such font covers, all of them capable of manufacture at small cost.

By the temporary cross, I hope it is not supposed that I mean only or mainly the timid floral cross which is allowed to stand where the sign of redemption should always be found, between the altar lights, but rather a *tentative* cross, whether hung at the chancel arch, or placed upon a screen that lacks its Rood. Here, since a screen does not inevitably *imply* a Rood, the occasional or periodic introduction of a temporary cross need not indicate a hesitating or temporizing policy. But it is a perfectly fair trial to see if it looks well, and if, in the best sense of the word, "it pleases the people."

In using such temporary crosses (as with the font covers) it will be wise to try several sizes and shapes; and probably before long, the desire for a permanent version will find both ways and means prepared.

But of all temporary structures, the screen is the most useful and the most advisable. It is hard to guess the best and seemliest form and size of a chancel screen until one has erected it, and then it is too late; but a few experiments and the few shillings expended in them will certainly not be thrown away. The common or vulgar objections to screens are that they stop the view, or make the Church look smaller, or that they are Popish. The last objection is, perhaps, the simplest to disprove, though the hardest to dispel. Of all things abhorred by the modern Roman Church, the screen is the greatest abomination. Of all old landmarks removed, the screen is the chiefest example. I should say that of old screens abroad, probably nine out of every ten have been ruthlessly abolished, while of modern Roman Churches in this country the proportion having screens is infinitesimally small. A *vista*, a *coup d'œil*, a "stately" altar; these are the desiderata. The second objection is only to be met by the direct negative. A screen does *not* make a Church look smaller, and the first may be dismissed almost in as many words. It does *not* stop the view except by the lower walls or panels, which, when a congregation is kneeling, certainly do hide the legs of clergy and choir, and to those near the front, the altar is often partially concealed as well. Yet, strange to say, the low wall or solid part of the screen is just the one part that no one objects to—provided always that there are no gates!!

To form a temporary screen, a few uprights of deal, 2 in. × 1 in., (narrow side placed east and west), a top "beam," say an inch plank about 3 in. wide, and a few pieces of stout wire or hoops sawn into pieces with which to make the cusps; these, with a few thin laths, a few nails, and some wire, complete the outfit of the screen-builder.

Having framed and tied together the lines required, they must be carefully and neatly covered with box or yew, the greatest care being taken that the posts are not *thicker* than permanent ones of oak would be. The lower part or wall of the screen should be about 3 ft. 6 in. high, and should be filled in solid with flannel or serge or dark linen. It is important that the base should be so treated, or it is not giving the screen a true experiment. And, if ever a permanent one replaces it, the objector could fairly say, "The other one didn't hide the view like this one does."

Temporary dossals or reredoses are, I fear, hopeless, save as the veriest templates or *silhouettes* of what is to be attempted. It may be worth while to cut out a frame of the same size as an intended triptych, and cover it with dark cloth, but to attempt to give any impression of a sculptured reredos in evergreens and laths, is too heavy a tax on the imagination.

The nearest approach to a temporary reredos that occurs to me as legitimate, is to "panel" the whole wall space at the east end by uprights of evergreen, with little arches suggested by the hoops and wires as already described for the screens, or to diaper the space with a continuous pattern, after the manner of fig. 4, Plate IV.

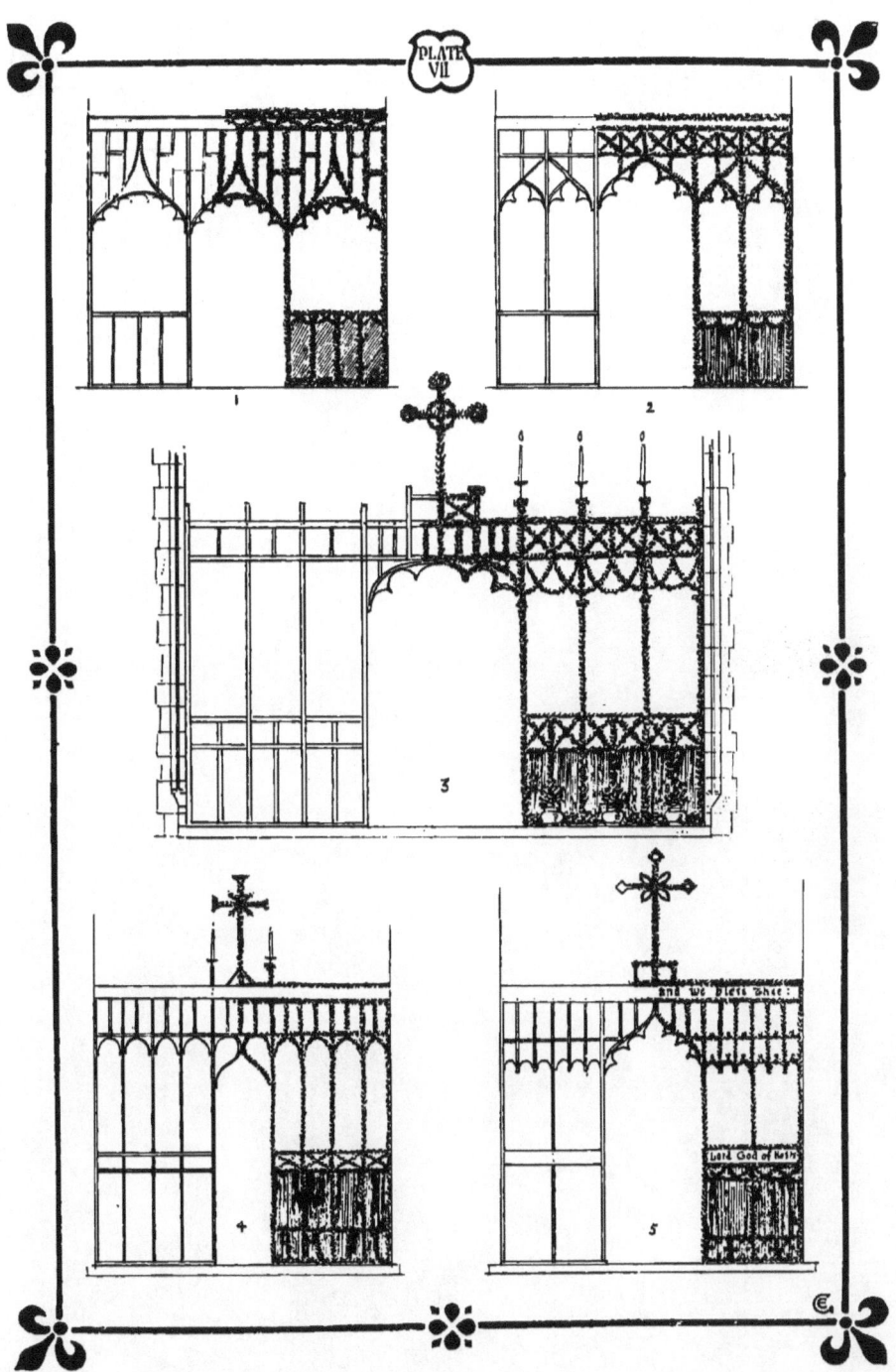

CHAPTER VII.

Of Banners.

NOTHING more decorative and festal can be used than banners and flags and pennons, if they are of good material and design. Nothing more utterly tawdry and meretricious, more absolutely below the dignity of GOD'S House, can be conceived than the things one commonly sees employed.

For a parish tea or a Sunday School fête paper flags are harmless enough, but to hang them in the sanctuary, touching an alabaster retable, to glue them on a pulpit of oak or cedar or walnut, to hang them round the neck of a brass eagle, and so on, is to sink to a depth of incongruity for which no words can be found.

When banners can be afforded of rich embroidery of silk and velvet, let us have them by all means for use in processions, and to hang upon the walls.

When we can get them of good and solid material, even without embroidery, we may still use them for wall decoration, and suspend them from the roof with good effect and good taste; but short of that, let us clear out all such things and have none of them.

But, it will be objected, how many Churches can afford decorative banners of any more precious material than stamped calico and cut out flock and American cloth?

I reply, most of us can afford them, and if not, we must do without until we can.

Plain white silk is not an unattainable luxury, and on this can be painted any design we wish; or, if silk is not within our means, *excellent* banners can be made of soft canvas, on which the richest figure work can be executed in gold and colour. In many ways these are better than silk; they are stronger and firmer in texture, and are also far more lasting.

Supposing, then, that a canvas banner is to be used, the shape should be marked out first, and then the banner should be pinned down on a drawing-board to keep it straight. A light coat of size will prevent the paint from running. The painting may be executed in either of two ways: (*a*) outlined in dark brown (burnt umber or bistre) and shaded in monochrome, and then the colouring can be put as a transparent "glaze;" or (*b*) the design can be painted solid in opaque colour. When the painting is finished the banner can be cut out and the edges bound with braid or gimp. Either a lining can be put as the backing, or the back itself can be painted in the same way as the front.

Such a banner as this may be the simplest emblem painted on a streamer of silk or canvas; or it may be a figure subject, a group of angels, or whatever you like. If it is well painted it is good enough to go anywhere, and far better even for processional use than a cheap and gaudy piece of shop embroidery.

A series of small bannerettes, or pennants hanging from the roof, either suspended by a cross bar, or projecting from the wall plate on a "spear," as in Westminster Abbey and S. George's, Windsor, will do more to decorate a Church than a hundred of such things hung flat on the walls. On blank spaces, however, at the east end or elsewhere, banners can be hung as pictures, flat against the wall.

For the small bannerettes, emblems of the passion, of the apostles and the saints, are appropriate, but for larger banners on the wall, either single figures or subjects are more suitable.

Some amateurs are, of course, quite capable of executing these, but generally, I think, an artist had better be called in.

Another development of the banner is a very favourite decoration now in Spain and South America, as formerly it undoubtedly was in most places, that is, to hang long streamers of damask silk, or velvet, or tapestry, down the walls and columns.

In many Spanish Churches it is the *only* decoration for festivals, since even flowers on the altar are practically unknown. From the top of the columns, or the cornice of the Church, enormous "blinds" are unrolled and fall to the ground. These are perfectly straight and square and smooth, exactly (as I say) like window blinds; but of the richest and most splendid silk or velvet.

The architecture of our English Churches does not so readily adapt itself to this form of decoration, but still a "mat" of tapestry, or of damask, fringed and bordered, will often hang well and give warmth and beauty to a blank space between windows and elsewhere.

But here again the decorator will complain, "Where does our work come in?" to which I would reply, the field is practically inexhaustible. There are endless diaper patterns of simple or intricate character only waiting to be copied. On Plate IX. there are a few reproduced from my collection, and hundreds of others are to be found and copied. Draw some of these out to scale, and of a good *large* size, and then see how you can transfer them to your square wall banner. There are three courses open to you : the first is to stencil the pattern on, having cut your design out in strong cartoon paper, thoroughly sized with Japanners' "gold-size" or painters' "knotting." For this it is necessary that your pattern be cut very true, so that all the "repeats" fit each other, and then before applying the stencil you must have guide lines of pencil or chalk ruled on to the surface of the fabric. This fabric I suppose for stencilling purposes to be *canvas*, already coloured or gilt. Having stencilled your pattern all over the piece, you will simply have to mount and fringe it, using a very narrow worsted braid and fringe, and it is ready for use.

The second plan is to *trace* your pattern on, and then paint it by hand.

The third plan is to employ appliqué, that is, the superimposing of one

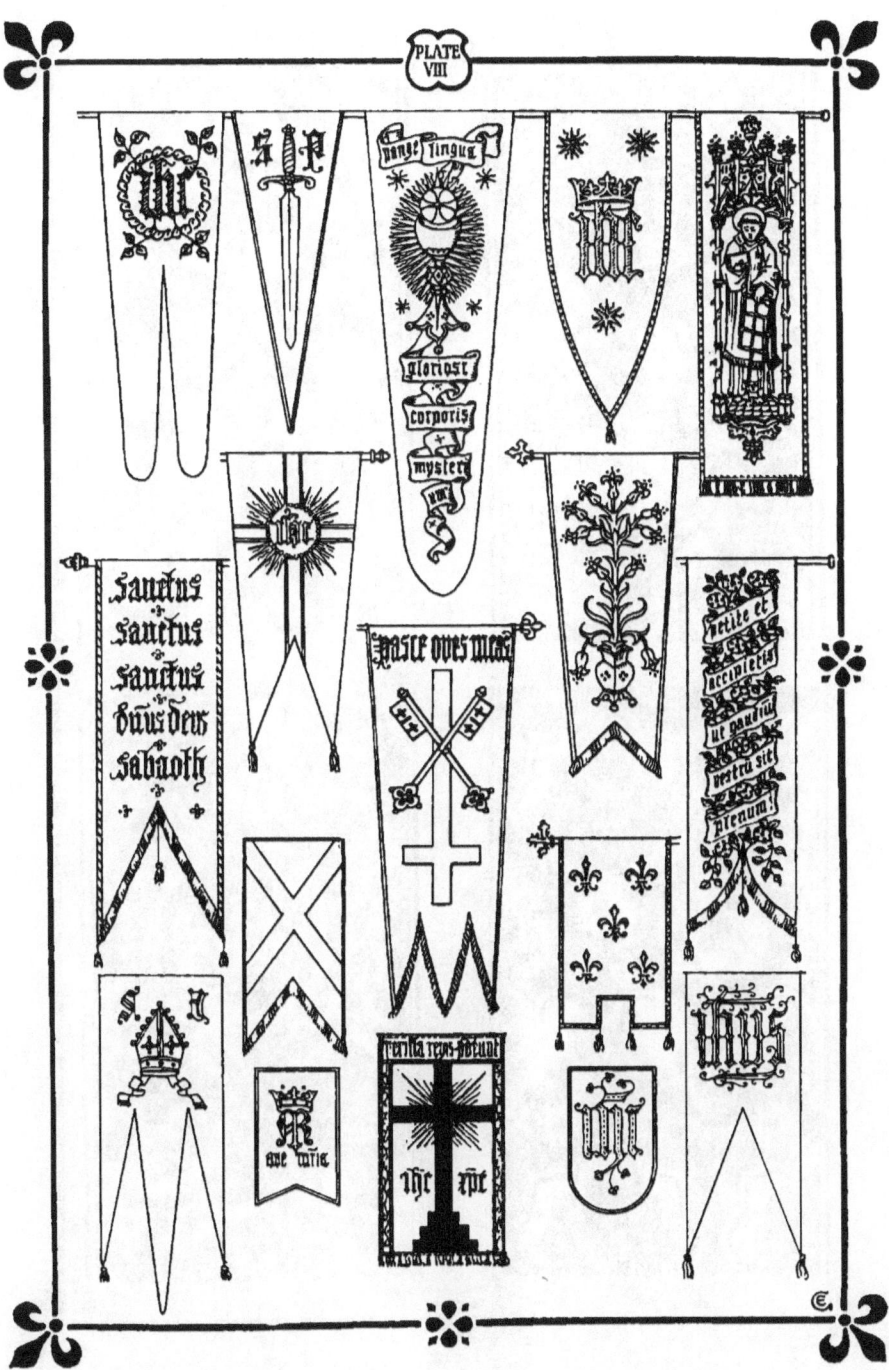

material on another. An appliqué of cotton, velvet, or silk, or fine cloth fastened to either canvas or silk or cloth, in the form of a diaper pattern, will be a rich and worthy hanging for a wall space.

Perhaps I cannot do better than give the following extract from *Church Embroidery*, by Mrs. Dolby, by way of description:—

"TO PREPARE VELVET, CLOTH, AND CLOTHS OF GOLD AND SILVER FOR APPLIQUÉ.

"Strain a piece of rather thin holland of about 1s. per yard—*not Union*—tightly in a frame, and cover it all over with 'embroidery paste,' carefully removing even the most minute lump from the surface. Upon this pasted holland, while wet, lay the piece of velvet or other material of which the appliqué is to be, smoothing it over the holland with a soft handkerchief to secure its even adhesion everywhere. If there be a necessity for drying quickly, place the frame upright at a distance of four feet from the fire, holland side to the stove. But it is always best, if possible, to *prepare* the material the day before using, that it may dry naturally, the action of the fire being likely to injure some fabrics as well as colours. The velvet, when perfectly dry, will be found tenaciously fixed to the holland, and may be removed from the frame.

"Now the entire design, or that portion of it intended to be formed of this material, is to be pounced through its pricked pattern on the holland side of the velvet, and traced correctly with a soft black-lead pencil; then cut out with sharp strong nail scissors, and it will be ready for applying to the article it is designed to ornament."

The embroidery paste alluded to is made in the following manner:—Take three table-spoonfuls of flour, and as much powdered resin as will lie on a shilling; mix them smoothly with half a pint of water, pour into an iron saucepan, and stir till it boils. Let it boil five minutes; then turn it into a basin, and when quite cold it is fit for use.

Shoemakers' or bookbinders' paste will serve more or less the same purpose; so, too, will some of the "fixers" for photographic mounting, but they are very expensive when used in bulk.

Emblems and devices of all sorts can be appliqué upon bannerettes, or on the centres of the quatrefoils described above. The process is good and honest, the effect is free from all pretence or sham; and though the patterns of diapers, perhaps, could be procured in fairly cheap hangings, and the emblems, no doubt, be bought ready printed, I hope my readers will prefer to work such things with their own hands, and not depend upon the printing press or the loom for their designs.

For the more skilful, dossals of appliqué, with painted panels of canvas, scroll-work, and shields or figures of saints and angels may afford the opportunity for good work. Here, however, I think the professional hand had better be invoked. Much meritorious amateur work is rendered hopelessly unsuitable, for want of the little extra knowledge which professional experience alone can give. Jarring styles, contradictory scales, and want of proportion, are enough to ruin the work of a Boticelli and an Albert Dürer when forced into collision.

Yet the amateur seems, as a rule, entirely oblivious to the claims of congruity. Four Fra Angelico's angels, alternating with Ruben's "Descent from the Cross," Raphael's "Holy Family," and Albert Dürer's "Annunciation," form a "reredos" entirely satisfying to the mind of the average "country parson" and his family.

CHAPTER VIII.

On the use of Texts.

THE 82nd Canon of 1603, among other directions, requires that there be "chosen sentences written upon the walls of Churches in places convenient."

Appropriate texts and legends are among the most effective of festival decorations; as also they are valuable "silent preachers," in the more permanent form contemplated by the framers of the Canon.

The best known of these is the Decalogue, which, with the Creed and LORD'S Prayer, was formerly of almost universal occurrence in Parish Churches, but not in Cathedrals or Collegiate buildings. The reason of this is clear. In days when *books* were scarcer even than *readers*, it was most convenient that those things which "every Christian should know for his soul's health" should be ever before his eyes.

Until a comparatively recent date these sentences were boldly printed in black and white, and were *legible*. But in the earlier days of the Tractarian and Ecclesiological movement, when an incalculable amount of destruction was perpetrated with the best intention and the worst results; many people, failing to find any ancient precedent, framed the commandments in a "reredos," and by dint of illumination and "compression" made them as good (or bad) as non-existent.

In the next stage of architectural progress, the commandments were banished, and at the present time but a small percentage of new or restored Churches possess them.

The argument against them is (*a*) they are not mediæval, and consequently, if over the altar, they are out of accord with a Gothic reredos. (*b*) They are no longer needed, since all men have books.

But on the other hand, since they are ordered by the Canon, it is perhaps hardly wise to omit them, and there is certainly one very appropriate position which they may well occupy, *i.e.*, in that part of the Church where the *children* sit, be it west or east. There is a special fitness, moreover, if they are put near the font, so that the prayer, faith, and obedience of the baptized may stand as a constant reminder of the Christian profession.

Beyond these well-known "texts" there are many others which are equally suitable for temporary or lasting decoration. Any one of the canticles may be written continuously round the walls or on the cornice; the *Benedictus* or *Magnificat*, the *Benedicite* or *Te Deum* will never weary the eye or heart of the reader.

For a Harvest Festival the Psalm *Jubilate* may be divided into short verses and placed in the window sills round the Church. (Or Psalms cxlvii., cxlviii., cl.)

Or in Lent the *Miserere* or *De profundis* may be used in the same way.

It is a question, not lightly to be settled or taken as universally applicable, whether these texts should be in Latin or English, and whether (whichever tongue is chosen) they should be written in Roman or Gothic lettering.

Possibly it may be thought unadvisable to employ aught but English in country places, while Latin *may* be used in town.

As to the condemnation of the Gothic character on the score of illegibility, it should be remembered that a large number of titles and headings in ordinary books and newspapers are so written; that there is certainly not a railway station or hoarding but has several such inscriptions in the way of advertisement; and as there is no question of which is the more beautiful, it seems a pity to throw away the old text, and by so doing render its chances of survival smaller.

It may interest the reader to know that the following newspaper headings contain the *whole alphabet* from a to z :—𝕸𝖔𝖗𝖓𝖎𝖓𝖌 𝕻𝖔𝖘𝖙, 𝕯𝖆𝖎𝖑𝖞 𝕹𝖊𝖜𝖘, 𝕼𝖚𝖊𝖊𝖓, 𝕱𝖎𝖊𝖑𝖉, 𝕰𝖝𝖈𝖍𝖆𝖓𝖌𝖊 𝖆𝖓𝖉 𝕸𝖆𝖗𝖙, 𝕵𝖔𝖍𝖓 𝕭𝖚𝖑𝖑, 𝕰𝖆𝖘𝖙 𝕶𝖊𝖓𝖙 𝕬𝖉𝖛𝖊𝖗𝖙𝖎𝖟𝖊𝖗.

Suppose, however, a mission room in London, with nothing ecclesiastical in its form or furniture save the altar, there, without question, good bold Roman type will tell the tale most readily.

TEXTS FOR TEMPORARY DECORATION.

The plan usually adopted by the well-intentioned amateur is to cut out the letters for a text in coloured paper or cloth, and paste them on a strip of another colour, which is then nailed to the wall.

This, however, save for the "flimsiest" and most passing occasion, such as a Sunday School feast, is neither beautiful nor worthy of the house of GOD.

If a text is worth *reading* it is worth *writing*, and the extra trouble involved is well expended.

If the illuminator feels unequal to the task of drawing a suitable alphabet, probably those given on Plates X., XI., and XII. will be of service; or letters of proper shape can be obtained and traced round before being coloured.

The groundwork of these texts may be of stout cartridge paper or painted canvas (or American cloth); or they may be of a more permanent character— boards of smoothly painted wood.

If, however, the decorators allow themselves the licence of coloured cloth (red or otherwise) for their texts, then the letters must be *cut out* in cardboard and tacked on to the ground; but in this case the foundation must be a thin wooden board, or the whole text will droop and sag. It may be said here that the *worst* possible foundation for a text is zinc or tin. This is a most useful material for cutting out small frames and emblems, to be covered with evergreen or moss, but it is, or should be, inadmissible for any other purpose. The surface "cockles," the paint cracks, and, worst of all, some one is sure to say when such a text is up: "It has cost too much to sacrifice it; let it stay."

In order that texts may look well, it is absolutely essential that all the letters should be upright and properly spaced out; and to insure this, the material on which the letters are to be fixed should be arranged on a long bench or table— a school desk for instance will serve. If the text is one of applied letters, fastened to cloth, they should *all* be laid out in their proper places before any of them are fastened down. It is a good plan to rule a few pencil lines at the top and bottom of the letters; and in fixing them, to insure their being upright, either to use a T or set square, or what will answer as well, a square piece of cardboard laid on the pencil line, so that its edge will give a right angle. The necessity of keeping the letters both upright and equidistant must be strongly urged. It frequently occurs that work, which has evidently cost much time and attention, is completely spoiled by want of regularity.

After the letters have been fixed on the groundwork they should be surrounded by a border. This may be made either of evergreens, with everlasting or other flowers introduced at intervals; or it may be painted on canvas or paper. A few simple designs of such borders are given on Plate XIII.

A plan frequently adopted is to cover cardboard letters with evergreens, and fasten them to the wall separately; but the objection to this plan is, that there is a great risk of defacing the plaster by the number of tacks or nails that have to be used in fixing. The better plan is to use a board that has been covered with white or coloured paper, and then, when the letters have been put on, to surround the whole with a narrow border, consisting of small sprigs of box or other evergreens, of which the leaves are quite small. The advantage obtained by this plan is, that the board can then be suspended in the required position upon two nails, which, besides avoiding the risk of injury to the walls above alluded to, also saves a great deal of time and trouble in fixing.

The various methods above described chiefly apply to the cutting out one material and laying it on another; but where the aid of painting is attainable, a much larger field is open, and greater variety of treatment, both as regards design and colour.

For those who have not had much experience in illuminated decorations, it is best to procure pots of colours already prepared for use, which can be thinned with a little turpentine if found to be too thick.

The best groundwork for these decorations is "prepared cloth," a material which is painted and prepared for decoration in the same way as canvas for oil painting.

Decorations done on such cloth, if carefully rolled round wooden rollers when put away, will last for years.

PLATE XI

AabBcdCefgD
EhijFGklmN
JnokpqLrM
NsOtuVvw
QryzK·S·L·V
W·X·Y·Z· Anno
Dñi Mcccxciij ✠

PLATE XII

Out of the
BCDEF
GHIKL I
MNOPQ
RSTUVWXY
Z · april the · A

When a cheaper material is required, white glazed buckram calico can be used, the process of painting being the same; or one may use strong continuous cartridge, which can be bought of any width and any length up to a score or so of yards.

If paper is employed, the colours, of course, will have to be water-colours, otherwise the process of application is the same.

When the material on which the text is to be written has been extended on a board or table, and the text spaced out, so as to obtain the proper distances between each word, the cardboard letter previously described should be laid upon it, and marked out with a black-lead pencil, care being taken to get a clear and distinct outline, and to keep the letters regular.

This being done, the next process is to fill in all the letters with their proper colours, using a camel hair, or sable brush, and putting only enough paint to cover the groundwork.

Should any gold letters or ornament be required, the leaf gold is the best to use, and the most durable. It is sold in books, and in order to apply it properly, a gilder's cushion, knife, and brush are required, as well as gold size. The size should be laid on the parts to be gilt, and when it is *almost* dry, it should be breathed upon to ensure its being sufficiently "sticky," then lay out a leaf of gold on the cushion and cut it with the knife to the required shape. This should be taken up with the gilder's brush and applied, care being taken that the parts are well covered with the leaf; then rub them gently over with a piece of cotton wool to remove all superfluous gold. An outline of black or red round the gold greatly improves the appearance of the gilded letters or ornament. "Transfer gold leaf" has been lately introduced, specially for amateurs' use; it is mounted on paper and can be cut with scissors. The work to be gilt is sized in the usual way, and the sheet laid upon it; the paper will peel off and leave the gold.

If the texts are not intended to be kept from year to year, and gold leaf is considered either too expensive or too troublesome to be used, bronze powder can be substituted. The work should be prepared with gold size in the way before described, and the powder, which will only adhere to the parts sized, may then be dusted on.

Where gold leaf is used, a good effect is produced by having a shaped patch at the commencement of the text, on which to place its initial letter, with some fine lines of ornament, in the style of the old illuminated missals.

I fear that it is too much to expect my readers to sign a pledge of total abstinence from gilt paper, Epsom salts, and cotton wool. Would, however, that I could do so! Imitation holly berries, straw paper, and glass powder I would include in the same condemnation, as being all utterly unfit for the sanctuary of the GOD of Truth.

It may be said that the Epsom salts "sparkle like frost," and the cotton wool is "just like snow." Very true, but one wants neither frost nor snow inside a weather-tight building, be it Church or home.

Everlasting flowers are perfectly legitimate for sacred use, provided they are not dyed violet and scarlet and magenta, and so rendered *false*. I know of no good reason against the natural everlastings being placed in the altar vases, or anywhere in Church. They are true flowers, grown in the garden of the LORD.

If, therefore, the patience of the worker will allow of a whole text being formed of everlastings, or holly berries, sewn on to a firm foundation, and put in a safe and suitable position, I see no cause to condemn the work.

At the same time there is no doubt that the most effective, the most beautiful and restful inscriptions are those, whether lasting or temporary, that are simply painted in one colour (preferably black) with, perhaps, red initials or border lines. Nothing is more senseless than a text of half-a-dozen words painted in as many colours, nor anything more aggravating and disturbing to a would-be worshipper. The capitals should be as few as possible. Every letter rising above the line destroys the continuity, and no one can have failed to notice in old work how scarce any but small letters are employed. In Latin, *deus* is not written with a large D, nor does *ego* stand out as with us, the self-assertive first person singular.

We should certainly, for the sake of appearance, never put a large letter where a small one will serve.

Supposing the alphabets on Plates X., XI., and XII. are used, and it is wished to enlarge them, this can be done by the usual method of ruling a sheet of paper into squares, and taking as many of them as are requisite to form letters of the same

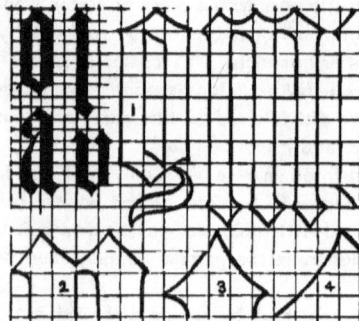

proportion as those of the chosen alphabet. The accompanying diagram explains the method of enlarging or reducing, by taking 1, 2, 3 or 4 diameters for the altered dimension. There is no fixed proportion between height and width, and therefore a letter may be lengthened or shortened "according to taste;" but so far as *thickness* of the lettering is concerned, bear in mind that the normal proportion of old text is about equal spaces of black and white—the space between each upright being about the same as the width of the upright. The nearer our text approaches this proportion the better and more decorative it looks.

Contractions in old inscriptions, whether English or Latin, often puzzle the lay mind; and although I should not recommend the employment of this short and easy method of saving labour, still it may be useful to give the main and best-known contractions, such as many of my readers have, no doubt, seen on brasses or paintings in their own parish Church.

In the first place, the "catechetical letters," * N or M, are the common

---

* N. or M., by the way, is probably a misprint for N. or NN., *nomen vel nomina*.

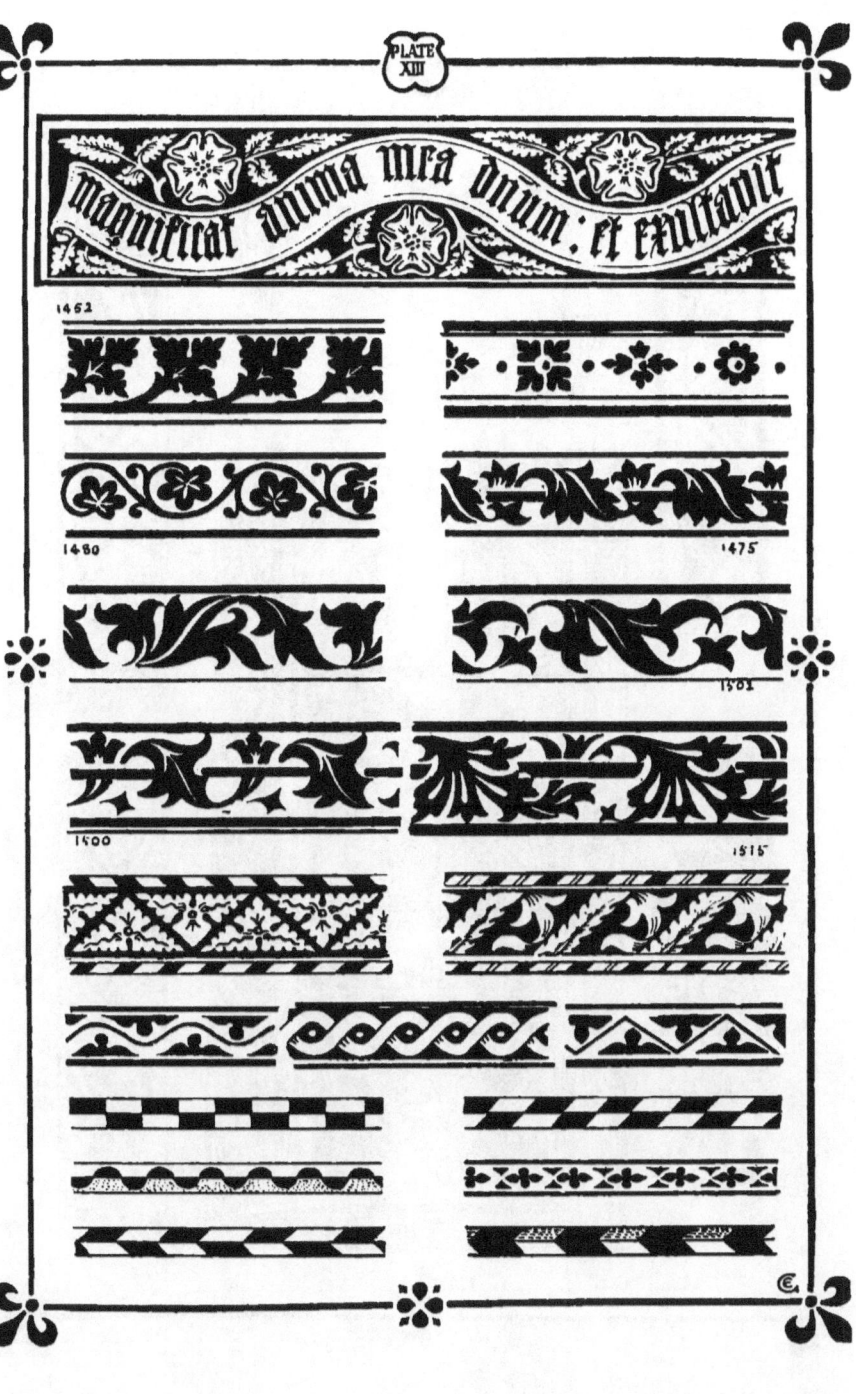

On the use of Texts.

victims of contraction. They are as often as not elided, and their place marked by a "slur;" but, the accompanying cess does not stop syllables disappear, a mere symbol. once learned it be- tively easy for the even to read an old truly some of the context to decipher. as will be seen in examples, the pro- here, but whole to be replaced by When these are comes compara- man in the street inscription, though words need the G, surmounted by a little º, is *rather* a free rendering of *ergo*, and QR. for *quia* recalls the mnemonic and phonetic atrocities of lecturers on shorthand and long memory.

Naturally the better known a word was, the more it was contracted. So, for instance, sanctus became sctus., scus., scs., or s. ; animae, aiae., aie. ; dominus, dnus., or d.

The choice of texts must rest with the readers and not the writer of this book, but in the hope of suggesting really appropriate "words in season" I here append a somewhat lengthy collection.

No "chapter and verse" are given ; firstly, because I give credit for a reasonable acquaintance with sacred writ ; but secondly, lest any should think it necessary or seemly to give the reference, in executing the work itself. To me it is simply irritating to see such words as these, with the reference appended :

I am the True Vine. Joh. xv. i.

No one would dream of looking up the quotation to test its accuracy, nor do the figures convey the slightest information or instruction.

Some of the "texts" in the following list are from the Prayer Book, and a few from the old office hymns of the Church ; but whatsoever they are, and whence they come, they are, it is to be hoped, suitable for common use. A Cruden's *Concordance* will supply as many more as may be wanted, either by way of addition or substitution.

There is one other sort of text to be mentioned—the *memorial*, whether of a fact, an event, or a person.

Here we have the voice of antiquity in our favour as to the use, but sternly against us as to our abuse of these memorials.

The abolition of intra-mural burial has practically taken from us the "brass." I mean the employment of that memorial of unequalled beauty, the engraved plate upon the floor, of which we have still so many in England left undesecrated by the impious hands of paid "reformers and informers," the Cromwells and the Dowsets of the Deformation, who did their best to break down all the houses of God in the land. There is not much sense now in putting a brass on the floor where no one *is* buried, or on the wall, where no one *could* be buried ; and so we have flown to the brass plate of commerce, usually the most hideous and offensive disfigurement that can be conceived—an oblong plate with "Gothic" letters of red and black (surrounded by a red border for 10s. extra); when new, shining like a looking-glass, when old, a dead black patch upon the wall; or, worse still, screwed on to a pulpit, soldered into a font, stuck on a reading-desk, plugged into the plaster or the stonework of a window: anywhere and everywhere a blot and an eyesore. This for two reasons, (*a*) because people desire to make the "brass" obvious; (*b*) because they wish to crowd on to it an amount of family history, that cannot be of the slightest interest to anyone save those who know it already!

Do not let it be supposed that I condemn the use of a memorial, even of brass, but it must not be the brass of Southampton Street. A narrow strip, not more than perhaps four inches wide, with a plain continuous text upon it, may fitly be placed, simply as a *record*, not an *advertisement*, on or near a memorial pulpit, or font, or screen; but only placed where it does *not* meet the eye of one entering the Church.

Orate pro aia. Joh. Smith qui obiit. Jan. 2, 1896: a-aetatis suae 75° ✠

This is more or less what "John Smith's window" would have had by way of inscription, had he lived 400 years ago; but now, after his name and titles, his age and birth-place, it would stand perhaps thus:—

In ever-loving
Memory,
and as a token of undying affection
and lasting grief,
his sorrowing
widow
Has dedicated this window (representing
the taking up into Heaven of Elijah)
TO THE CHURCH
in which he worshipped
40 years.

Who can fail to be touched by the simple appeal for mercy to JESUS, and the request for our prayers that meets our eyes when we look down upon a mediæval tomb, or to contrast it with the bombast and display of modern records? A few suggestions are here given of brief inscriptions which may suffice to record gifts.

Servus Dei d.d. (date).
In honorem Dei et usum ecclesiæ (date).
In mem. Joh. Smith (date).
a.m.d.g. d.d. ✠.S. (date).
Deo gratias (date).
Quid retribuam domino.

Or it may be that the shield of arms (with the donor's initials) would serve as well or better; doubtless found on ancient fonts were intended as marks of gift.

Or if the inscription foot of a pulpit, this may serve as a hint.

Volumes might be written on this head, but there are other memorial texts to be noticed.

The record of the con-secration, restoration, or enlargement of the Church, or a part of it, may be made in many ways: (a) by a carved inscription upon a stone, inside or out, *flush* with the wall, and not a "tablet;" or (b) the record may be fixed on glazed tiles and built in. Such an example, by the way, exists in Malvern Abbey. Another form of memorial is the chronogram, a verse, text, or rhyme, of which, every letter having a *numerical* value being added to the rest, gives the date.

Two huge volumes of *Chronograms, Ancient and Modern*, published by Elliott Stock, will give the reader a thousand examples; but, as I know to my cost, every man must invent his own, and the difficulty is obvious. Your inscription must not have more than one M, or you run to 2000 A.D. at a leap; nor is it safe to use too many D's, as each = 500. Perhaps I may be pardoned for giving one example of my own, as showing the method and point of a chronogram. Long ago, a Church tower had fallen and broken all its bells. I was called in to rebuild it, and having done so, cut into a band of stone beneath the bell-chamber these words:—

ECCE : tUrrIs : oLIM : STRATA :
DEO : rUrsUs : eXORNATA :
RESONANTI : VoCE : GRATA.

Here CC + V + I + L + I + M, etc., etc., = 1883.

I recommend this interesting exercise of ingenuity to my more *patient* readers, and *only* those.

CHAPTER IX.

On the Choice of Texts for the various Seasons.

ADVENT.

"He cometh to judge the earth."
"Prepare ye the way of the LORD."
"Behold, thy King cometh unto thee."
"Be ye also ready. The Son of man cometh."
"The Son of man shall come in His glory."
"O come, O come, Emmanuel."
"Leva Jerusalem, oculos tuos."
"Veni Domine visitare nos in pace."
"Tu es qui venturus es."
"The night is far spent, the day is at hand."
"The LORD is at hand."
"Who may abide the day of His coming."
"The day of the LORD so cometh as a thief in the night."
"The day of CHRIST is at hand."
"Behold, He cometh with clouds; and every eye shall see Him."
"Surely I come quickly; even so, come, LORD JESUS."
"He shall come again in His glorious majesty to judge both the quick and the dead."
"Behold a virgin shall bear a son."

CHRISTMAS.

"There shall come a Star out of Jacob, and a Sceptre shall rise out of Israel."
"The right hand of the LORD bringeth mighty things to pass."
"The people that walked in darkness have seen a great light."
"Unto us a Child is born, unto us a Son is given."
"His name shall be called Wonderful, Counsellor, the Mighty GOD, the Everlasting FATHER, the Prince of Peace."
"There shall come forth a Rod out of the stem of Jesse, and a Branch shall grow out of his roots."
"The LORD, our Righteousness."
"The Desire of all nations shall come."
"Behold, thy King cometh."
"The Sun of Righteousness shall arise with healing in His wings."
"Thou shalt call His name JESUS."
"Emmanuel! GOD with us."
"Hosanna to the Son of David."
"Hosanna in the highest!"
"The day-spring from on high hath visited us."
"Behold, I bring you glad tidings of great joy."
"Unto you is born this day a SAVIOUR, which is CHRIST the LORD."
"Glory to GOD in the highest, on earth peace, good will toward men."
"Let us now go even unto Bethlehem."
"Let all the angels of GOD worship Him."
"He bringeth His First begotten into the world."
"Corde natus ex parentis."
"Gloria in excelsis Deo et in terra pax hominibus bonæ voluntatis."
"Videbitis regem regum procedentem a Patre tanquam sponsum de thalamo suo."
"Venite adoremus: ecce tabernaculum Dei cum hominibus."
"Hodie nobis de cœlo pax vera descendit."
"Verbum caro factum est."
"The Consolation of Israel."
"A Light to lighten the Gentiles."
"The Word was made flesh and dwelt among us."
"GOD sent forth His SON."
"GOD manifest in the Flesh."
"The Author of Salvation."
"The Finisher of Faith."
"We love Him because He first loved us."
"Now is come Salvation and Strength."
"King of kings and LORD of lords."
"The root and offspring of David, and the bright and Morning Star."
"GOD of GOD, Light of Light, Very GOD of Very GOD."
"GOD and Man: one CHRIST."
"Thou art the everlasting SON of the FATHER."
"Thou art the King of Glory, O CHRIST."

(The Circumcision.)

"His name was called JESUS."
"Circumcision is that of the heart."
"Oleum effusum nomen tuum."
"At the name of JESUS every knee shall bow."

EPIPHANY.

"The people that walked in darkness have seen a great light."
"He shall bring forth judgment to the Gentiles."
"The LORD shall be thine everlasting light."
"The Gentiles shall see Thy righteousness."
"The Gentiles shall come unto Thee from the ends of the earth."

On the Choice of Texts for the various Seasons.

EPIPHANY—(continued).

"Venit lumen tuum Jerusalem."
"Arise, shine, for Thy light is come."
"Omnes venient aurum et thus deferentes. Alleluia."
"We have seen His star in the East, and are come to worship Him."
"When they saw the star they rejoiced."
"They presented unto Him gifts; gold, frankincense, and myrrh."
"A light to lighten the Gentiles."
"Rejoice, ye Gentiles, with His people."

LENT.

"It is of the LORD's mercies that we are not consumed."
"The sacrifices of GOD are a broken spirit."
"GOD be merciful unto us."
"Have mercy upon us, O LORD."
"Fili dei miserere mei."
"Parce nobis Domine."
"De profundis clamavi."
"Turn us again, O LORD GOD of Hosts."
"Thou GOD of Hosts look down from Heaven."
"Spare thy people, good LORD."
"Turn ye then and ye shall live."
"Let the wicked forsake his way."
"His mercy is on them that fear Him."
"Have mynde, have mercy."
"By Thy fasting and temptation, Good LORD, deliver us." *
"Kyrie Eleison; Christe Eleison, Kyrie Eleison."

PASSIONTIDE.

"He was despised and rejected of men."
"With His stripes we are healed."
"He was wounded for our transgressions."
"It is finished."
"He humbled Himself to the death of the Cross."
"Thou hast brought me into the dust of death."
"Deus meus respice in me."
"His own self bare our sins in His own body on the tree."
"Behold my affliction."
"By Thy Cross and Passion, good LORD, deliver us."
"By Thy precious death and burial, good LORD, deliver us."
"Behold, and see if there is any sorrow like unto my sorrow."
"Is it nothing to you all ye that pass by?"
"O my people, what have I done unto you?"
"They crucified Him."
"They shall look on Him whom they have pierced."
"By His stripes we are healed."

EASTER.

"Death hath no more dominion over Him."
"I know that my Redeemer liveth."
"The LORD is King for ever and ever."
"He is risen."
"The LORD is risen indeed."
"I am the Resurrection and the Life."
"This JESUS hath GOD raised up."
"He whom GOD raised again saw no corruption."
"CHRIST was raised again for our justification."
"If we be dead with CHRIST, we believe that we shall also live with Him."
"CHRIST our Passover is sacrificed for us, therefore let us keep the feast."
"Now is CHRIST risen from the dead, the first-fruits of them that slept."
"As in Adam all die, even so in CHRIST shall all be made alive."
"This is the LORD's doing, and it is marvellous in our eyes."
"By man came Death, by man came also the Resurrection."
"Thou shalt not suffer Thine Holy one to see corruption."
"GOD is the LORD who hath showed us light."
"O death, where is thy sting? O grave, where is thy victory."
"Death is swallowed up in victory."
"Our life is hid with CHRIST in GOD."
"I am He that liveth, and was dead; and, behold, I am alive for evermore."
"LORD of lords, King of kings."
"Alleluia! Alleluia! Alleluia!"
"Alleluia! for the LORD GOD omnipotent reigneth."
"He is the very Paschal Lamb which was offered for us."
"Haec dies quam fecit Dominus: Exultemus et laetemur in ea. Alleluia."
"Resurrexit."
"Pascha nostrum."
"Lo, the winter is past."
"GOD hath fulfilled the promise, in that He hath raised up JESUS again."
"Peace be unto you."

ASCENSIONTIDE.

"Thou art gone up on High."
"Thou hast crowned him with glory and honour."
"The LORD sitteth a King for ever."
"Thou, LORD, art Most High for evermore."
"He was received up into heaven, and sat on the right hand of GOD."
"Videntibus illis elevatus est."
"Lift up your heads, O ye Gates, and be ye lift up, ye everlasting Doors, and the King of glory shall come in."

---

* So for Lent and Passiontide any of the penitential verses of the Litany may be fitly used, either in Latin or English.

ASCENSIONTIDE—(continued).

"The Son of man, which is in heaven."
"He was taken up, and a cloud received Him out of their sight."
"He ever liveth to make intercession for them."
"Thou sittest at the right hand of God."
"He ascended into heaven."
"Be Thou exalted, LORD, in Thine own strength."
"Set up Thyself, O GOD, above the Heavens, and Thy glory above all the earth."

ROGATIONTIDE.

"We wait for Thy loving-kindness, O LORD, in the midst of Thy Temple."
"Ask, and ye shall receive."
"LORD, teach us to pray."
"Thy blessing is upon Thy people."
"Thou that hearest the prayer, to Thee shall all flesh come."
"We beseech Thee to hear us, good LORD."
"LORD, hear our prayer, and let our cry come unto Thee."
"O CHRIST, hear us."
"O LORD, arise, help us, and deliver us for Thy Name's sake."
"Both now and ever vouchsafe to hear us."
"O LORD, let Thy mercy be showed upon us."
"Like as we do put our trust in Thee."

WHITSUNTIDE.

"The Comforter, which is the HOLY GHOST."
"They were all filled with the HOLY GHOST."
"The HOLY GHOST fell on all them that heard the word."
"The SPIRIT beareth witness, because the SPIRIT is Truth."
"Spiritus Domini replevit orbem terrarum."
"Spiritus qui a Patre procedit Ille me clarificat."
"Thou only, O CHRIST, with the HOLY GHOST, art most high in the glory of GOD the FATHER."
"The HOLY GHOST came down at this time from heaven."
"The HOLY GHOST, the LORD, and giver of life."
"Veni Creator Spiritus."

TRINITY SUNDAY.

"Holy, Holy, Holy, LORD GOD Almighty, which was, and is, and is to come."
"Not three GODS, but one GOD."
"Qualis Pater, talis Filius, talis Spiritus Sanctus: Haec est Fides Catholica."
"Unitas in Trinitate, et Trinitas in Unitate veneranda."
"The FATHER is GOD, the SON is GOD, and the HOLY GHOST is GOD."

TRINITY SUNDAY—(continued).

"We worship one GOD in Trinity, and Trinity in unity."
"Glory be to the FATHER, and to the SON, and to the HOLY GHOST."
"O holy, blessed, and glorious Trinity, three persons and one GOD."
"Gloria Patri et Filio et Spiritui Sancto: Sicut erat in principio et nunc et semper: et in saecula saeculorum."
"Sanctus: Sanctus: Sanctus."

HARVEST THANKSGIVING.

"While the earth remaineth, seed-time and harvest shall not cease."
"Man doth not live by bread alone, but by every word that proceedeth out of the mouth of the LORD."
"The earth is the LORD's, and the fulness thereof."
"Thou visitest the earth, and blessest it, Thou makest it very plenteous."
"Thou crownest the year with Thy goodness."
"Bless the LORD, O my soul, and forget not all His benefits."
"Wine maketh glad the heart of man, and bread strengtheneth man's heart."
"He maketh peace in thy borders, and filleth thee with the finest of wheat."
"Honour the LORD with thy firstfruits; so shall thy barns be filled with plenty."
"The harvest is the end of the world, and the reapers are the angels."
"The bread of life."
"In due season we shall reap, if we faint not."
"O all ye green things upon the earth, bless ye the LORD."

SCHOOL FEASTS.

"The fear of the LORD is the beginning of wisdom."
"Train up a child in the way he should go; and when he is old, he will not depart from it."
"Remember now thy Creator in the days of thy youth, while the evil days come not, nor the years draw nigh when thou shalt say, I have no pleasure in them."
"Suffer the little children to come unto me, and forbid them not: for of such is the kingdom of GOD."
"Feed My lambs."
"Children, obey your parents in the LORD: for this is right."
"Keep innocency, and hold fast the thing which is right, for that shall bring a man peace at the last."
"Come ye children and hearken unto me: I will teach you the fear of the LORD."

Beside the texts here given there are also many texts appropriate to the various *parts* of the building. As for example—

THE PORCH.

"This is none other than the House of God, and this is the gate of Heaven."
"I will offer in His tabernacle sacrifices of joy."
"The Lord loveth the gates of Zion."
"Hear ye that enter into the gate."
"I will come into Thy House."
"This is the gate of the Lord."
"Enter into His gates with thanksgiving, and into His courts with praise."
"Peace be within Thy walls."
"I was glad when they said unto me, Let us go into the House of the Lord."
"Rejoice within your gates."
"Come into His courts."

THE FONT.

"I acknowledge one Baptism for the remission of sins."
"Suffer the little children to come unto Me, and forbid them not : for of such is the kingdom of God."
"In nomine Patris et Filii et spiritus sancti."
"Petite et accipietis."
"Spiritus ubi vult spirat."
"With Thee is the well of life."
"He that believeth and is baptized shall be saved."
"Repent and be baptized."
"One Lord, one Faith, one Baptism."
"Ye must be born again."
"Haurietis aquas in gaudio de fontibus salvatoris."

ΝΙΨΟΝΑΝΟΜΗΜΑΜΗΜΟΝΑΝΟΨΙΝ.

This, it will be observed, reads indifferently from right to left, or *vice versa*, and should, perhaps, be placed so as to surround the font.

THE ROOD SCREEN

may well have a text running along its beam—

"Sic Deus dilexit mundum."
"O Saviour of the world, Who by Thy cross and precious blood hast redeemed us ; save us and help us, we humbly beseech Thee, O Lord."
"We adore Thee, O Christ, and we bless Thee, for by Thy holy cross Thou hast redeemed the world."
"O Lamb of God, that takest away the sins of the world, have mercy upon us."

"I, if I be lifted up, will draw all men unto Me."
"Come unto Me and I will give you rest."
"For the joy set before Him He endured the cross."
"We preach Christ crucified."
"He made peace by the Blood of His cross."
"Regnavit a ligno Deus."
"Per proprium sanguinem introivit semel in sancta."
"By Me, if any man enter in : He shall be saved."

ON THE RETABLE,

we may often place words appropriate to the subject depicted, as under a crucifixion any of the texts given above for the rood, or some of the following :—

"Ever since the world began hath Thy seat been prepared."
"I will give to eat of the Tree of Life."
"Deliciae meae cum filiis hominum."
"We give thanks to Thee for Thy great glory."
"The memorial of Thine abundant kindness shall be showed."

"Behold the tabernacle of God is with men."
"Quos Sanguis Dirus Christi Dulce Divine Lavit."
"Pange Lingua Gloriosi corporis mysterium."

ON THE ORGAN.

"Let everything that hath breath praise the Lord."
"Venite exultemus Domino."
"Te Deum laudamus."
"Benedicite omnia opera Domini Domino."
"Laudate eum in chordis et organo."

"O praise God in His Holiness."
"Sing unto the Lord and praise His Name."
"My mouth shall speak the praise of the Lord."
"Make a joyful noise unto the Lord."
"Rejoice and sing praise."

72   A Manual of Church Decoration and Symbolism.

These texts are but a tithe, or rather a hundredth part of the words of sacred writ that may suitably be employed, either for temporary or permanent decoration, to stir up the minds of God's people by way of remembrance. They are rather given by way of suggestion than dictation; and the storehouse itself, the Bible, is in the hands of all.

On the Position of Texts.

With the natural perversity that characterizes our race, we too frequently put our texts in just the wrong places: either where they are inappropriate, or impossible, or hard to read. The best posi- tion for legi- bility, I need hardly say, is the horizontal, yet that seldom pleases the ordi- nary decorator. Round an arch, (and the more pointed, the more accept- able) is where one naturally casts one's eyes to see the point selected by our pious sisters for our instruction. Rarely do they manage to strike the line of the archmould; hardly ever do they manage to divide the words

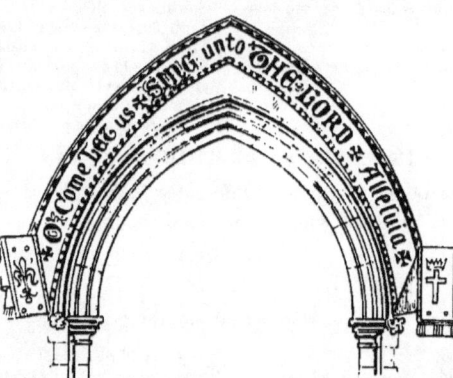

so that they in any way balance each other; and this sketch is by no means a caricature of the "pointed style" of textual instruction in common use. The best

places of all for texts are those level lines of the building usually devoid of ornament. The cornice or wall plate, the window sills, and the "beam out of the wall cry" for words in which they may take their share of teaching, in vain. There is no absolute objection to placing a text, whether temporary or lasting, over an arch, provided that it can be

read without ricking one's neck; and often a flat or slightly curved arch offers a perfectly legitimate opening for such decoration.

In both these cases it will be seen that the scroll is as legible as though it were on a line, but in these or other cases, unless the text is to ruin the appearance of the arch, it must follow the exact sweep of its radius. This is not always easy to get, and more often than not it will be found better to make the main scroll horizontal, with "flying" ends, as on fig. C.

If my readers will have texts over large and sharp-pointed arches, let me entreat them to employ a dependable carpenter or other fit person to take an exact template.

As to the position of texts, so far as their appositeness is concerned, never place words which manifestly refer to some other than the position occupied. For instance, to put, "Ye must be born again" over the altar, or, "Behold the Lamb of GOD" over the font, is obviously absurd. But the most terribly sad example of ill taste I ever saw was in a Suffolk Church, where, over a pew whose seat *backed* and almost touched the poor, mean altar rails, was inscribed, "Surely the LORD is in this place, and I knew it not!" So, too, I fancy I have seen in a tightly-shut and straitly-pewed Church, such words as these: "The rich and the poor meet *together*; the LORD is the maker of them all!" "*Freely* ye have received; freely give!"

PART II.

CHAPTER X.

On Emblems generally.

EMBLEMS or symbols are by no means all of one sort, but are more or less clearly to be classified under distinct headings.

(*a*) Some are purely SYMBOLICAL or allegorical: the pelican, or the phoenix, or the pomegranate, if taken as emblems of the LORD, are simply so taken as figuring some qualities recognised by the faithful as pertaining to CHRIST.

So with some of the saintly emblems: the burning heart of S. Augustine, or the beehive of S. Ambrose, and the two pillars of S. Athanasius, these figure not the deeds but the character of those signified.

(*b*) Others are DOCTRINAL: the Divine Hand, the interlaced triangles, or the shield of the Trinity, or the ΙΧΘΥΣ, for instance. These convey to us the faith of the Church.

(*c*) Again, there are those purely METAPHORICAL. We show our LORD as the Good Shepherd, because He said, "I *am* the Shepherd;" or as a rose, since He said, "I *am* the Rose;"* or the *Agnus Dei*, because the Baptist said, "Behold the Lamb of GOD."

(*d*) Then there is a very large class formed by such emblems as are intended to be distinctly HISTORICAL. Such are the saltire of S. Andrew, the wheel of S. Catharine, and the many other tokens of the sufferings of the saints. So the emblems of the Passion and the whole heraldry of the Cross fall under the same classification.

(*e*) There are, too, emblems OFFICIAL: the mitre, the Papal tiara, the helmet, the staff, the cope, the dalmatic, and a score of other badges of office are attributed to those who probably never wore the things at all, and certainly did not do so in the form portrayed. The first martyr, S. Stephen, did not wear a dalmatic with an apparelled alb; nor did S. Peter ever see a tiara or a patriarchal cross. But what can we do, save use the "signs of the times" we are working in, and be therewith content? I don't for a moment suppose, when designing an Athanasius, in a fifteenth century cope, with a legend in black letter, and a shaven face, surmounted by a jewelled mitre, that he ever looked a bit like that. But he does look like a bishop of the Catholic Church, and he fits in with his English surroundings when so depicted.

* Cant. ii. 1.

If realism be insisted upon, scarcely any representation will be possible; since we cannot be sure of the shape and pattern, the colour of the clothing: still less of the features, the beard, and hair of any early saint. Realism, too, would prohibit the attempt to show the sacred hierarchy of heaven, and we can only credit the angels, in their orders and courses, with the emblems, by common consent appropriate to their names and dignities.

(*f*) Other emblems are REPRESENTATIVE, not of the saints, but of their work or trade: the shoes of S. Crispin or the tent-maker's tools of Priscilla show their handicraft; while the fetters of S. Leonard show, not his own chains, but those worn by the recipients of his goodness.

(*g*) The next class would be described by heralds as CANTING. This unsavoury word, however, is not meant (even heraldically) in an invidious sense. Arms are called "canting," or *parlant*, when they form a *rebus*, or a play upon a name. A bolt in a tun for "Bolton," a man in a tree for "Manningtree," are, without question, of the same sort as S. Agnes' *lamb*, S. Cornelius' *horn*, and S. Sidwell's *scythe*.

What to say of S. Christopher I know not. Tradition says that he was a heathen giant Offero, but having "carried CHRIST" he became Christo-pher, and is so represented. Either the name gave the legend, or the legend the name—who can say?

(*h*) A last division may, perchance, be called TRADITIONAL, in its modern and false sense, i.e., something carried on from—nowhere! It would seem that there is neither rhyme nor reason for a large number of such emblems, save the individual fancy of some unknown artist, whom others followed blindly.

Books, which the holders never *wrote*, and probably never *read*, are, of course, merely vague and uncertain. But why S. John of Ely should have a sun and moon is more than one can tell. Certain it is that licence has been freely taken in this direction, and perchance it may be extended even to us, if we only avail ourselves of it when all else fails.

The general significance of the common emblems is something of this sort:

A CROSS signifies self-surrender, and acceptance of suffering, as in the case of S. Alban, S. Olave, S. Boniface, etc.

ARMOUR, the resistance to evil.

ARROWS, I fancy, are not always the actual implements of martyrdom, but sometimes show the fiery darts of the enemy, and the sharpness of the saint's sufferings. S. Augustine's arrows, at least, indicate no martyrdom.

AN ASPERGE is used as a token of purity and holiness of life. The saints generally figured with this emblem are S. Conrad, S. Benedict, S. Leo III., and S. Robert.

A BANNER, victory and triumph. As such it is borne by S. Michael, S. George, S. Victor, S. James Major, S. David the King, and S. Wenceslas.

A BASKET signifies liberality to the poor, e.g., S. Dorothy, S. Elizabeth, and S. Romanus.

A BEAR is the emblem of solitary life and self-restraint: so wild beasts of all sorts show the same, when surrounding S. Columban, S. Blaize, S. Anthony, S. Germanus, S. Gallus the Abbot, and other saints.

BEGGARS show the merciful charity of the saints, e.g., S. Elizabeth and S. Medard.

A BELL generally refers to some more or less known legend. The saints associated with this are S. Anthony, S. Gildas, S. Theodulus, and S. Benedict.

A BEE-HIVE is the sign of eloquence, as in the case of S. Ambrose, S. Bernard, and S. Chrysostom.

BELLOWS, the blasts of the devil's temptation, e.g., S. Genevieve.

BIRDS are often shown as messengers bringing some object to the saints: to S. Blaize, food; to S. Erasmus, a crown; to S. Oswald, a letter and a ring.

BOOKS ought to show authorship, but often they are intended to show love of study and the word of GOD. S. Matthew or S. Paul, of course, bear the books they *wrote*, but S. Anne, S. Margaret, and scores of others can only bear the book in token of their own learning, or, as in the case of S. Catharine, patronage of learning.

BREAD indicates charity to the poor, e.g., S. Nicholas, S. Elizabeth, and S. John of GOD.

A CANDLE is shown in the hand of S. Beatrice and S. Genevieve.

A CASKET as often as not shows the relics of the saint himself.

A CALDRON is the implement of martyrdom employed, e.g., S. John the Evangelist, S. Erasmus, S. Lucy, S. Boniface.

CHAINS.—Generally the tortures of the saint are indicated, as with S. Peter, or S. Ignatius; but with S. Leonard or S. Balbina they show the fetters of those aided by the saint.

A CHALICE, of course, is the sign of the priestly office, and especially after the twelfth century, when the cup was taken from the laity.

In the case of S. Thomas Aquinas it shows his writing on the mystery of the Sacrament.

When, however, a dragon, or spider, or snake is in it, the cup indicates escape from poisoning, as with S. John the Evangelist, S. Benedict; or poisoning, e.g., S. Edward, K.M.

THE HOLY CHILD is shown with many later saints, in token of chastity and gentleness of heart, e.g., S. Francis Assisi, S. Anthony of Padua.

A CHURCH indicates the foundation of a see or a monastery, e.g., S. Chad holds Lichfield.

A CITY refers to some notable defence or deliverance by the saint, as S. Lupus of Troyes, or S. Richard of Chichester.

A CLOAK in S. Martin's case records his charity, but generally it records the miracle of crossing the sea thereon instead of by a ship. S. Hyacinth, S. Sebald, and S. Raymond are those commonly so shown.

A CLUB often denotes martyrdom at the hand of "barbarous" heathen, as distinguished from more "legal" means. S. Nicomede, S. Lambert, S. Magnus, among others, bear this emblem.

A CROSS, if an official staff, shows the office of the bearer. A long, tall cross in other hands, indicates the preaching of the Gospel and stout witness for the faith.

A CROWN shows either royal or princely rank, as with S. Ethelburga, S. Hilda, S. Osyth, S. Edward, S. Edmund, S. Olave, and so on. Sometimes the title to it is extremely doubtful, as with S. Margaret and other female saints. But if it be not an earthly crown, that of martyrdom and celestial honour is indicated.

CRUCIFIXION.—Besides the authenticated martyrdom of many who followed our LORD'S way of sorrows, as S. Peter, S. Andrew, S. Denys, S. Symeon, and S. Julian, there is one extraordinary example of a *woman* (bearded and crucified), called S. Wilgefortis. No one has ever succeeded in clearing up this legend, which takes many forms, but if any of my readers should be puzzled by seeing the figure in a foreign Church, this is the name of it.

THE DAGGER, as an instrument of death, is borne by S. Edward, S. Olave, S. Agnes, S. Canute, and others.

DEVIL.—Sometimes in the form of a beast, and sometimes in his own, the devil often accompanies a saint. S. Anthony has a *goat ;* S. Demetrius, a *scorpion ;* S. Margaret, S. George, S. Michael, S. Sylvester, S. Martha, and S. Julian, a *dragon ;* with S. Bernard, S. Anthony, S. Bridget, S. Oswald, S. Dunstan, S. Gertrude, and S. Bartholomew the foul fiend appears in his own guise.

A DOG generally shows faithful service, by the animal, or possibly by some attendant. S. Bernard has a white dog ; S. Dominic, a dog with a flaming torch ; S. Roch, one with a loaf in his mouth.

A DOVE, usually on the shoulders, whispering in the ear of the saint, without question is the sign of inspiration, e.g., S. Hilary, S. Ambrose, S. Gregory the Great, and S. Basil.

In the case of S. Agnes, S. Cornelia, S. Teresa, it implies divine consolation.

AN EAGLE, the symbol of S. John the Evangelist, is also shown with S. Gregory the Great, S. Augustine of Hippo, and S. Medard.

AN EYE is the sign of torture by blinding, e.g., S. Lucy or S. Leger.

FETTERS are the emblems of S. Leonard, S. Quentin, and S. Egwyn.

FIRE is often shown at the side, beneath the feet, or over the head ; but in very few cases does it indicate martyrdom. S. Patrick, S. Vitus, S. Basil, S. Aidan, S. Boniface, and S. Thecla are so shown, but only in the latter case does it clearly indicate death by burning.

FISH, in the case of the Apostles, S. Andrew and S. Jude, refer to their trade, but in other cases they refer to some legend, often after the pattern of

S. Peter's fish with the coin. S. Benno, for instance, and S. Mauritius received keys from fish.

FLOWERS show generally some vision of the joys of Paradise. S. Cecilia, S. Dorothy, and S. Agnes are shown with flowers because of the foretaste of celestial joys vouchsafed to them in their sufferings.

FOUNTAINS.—Remembering our LORD'S words, that there should be living waters welling up to those who believed, it is not wonderful that fountains are often shown springing up before the saints whose faith has begotten faith in others. Especially is this the case with great missionaries like S. Boniface, S. Augustine, S. Ive, or S. Clement.

A GIRDLE of the Blessed Virgin is shown given to S. Thomas and S. Stephen, Abb. S. Margaret and S. Monica bear their *own* girdles.

THE GLOBE is the emblem of contempt of worldly honours. S. Francis and S. Bruno have it at their feet; S. Ladislas in his hand, signed with crosses; S. Ignatius also holds it.

A HEAD is often carried in the hands, either in addition to, or instead of, one upon the shoulders. S. Proculus, S. Dionysius, S. Winifred, S. Regula, S. Sidwell, and S. Osyth all carry their own heads, while S. Cuthbert is shown carrying S. Oswald's.

A HEART in the hand shows the love of the saint, answering to the love of the Sacred Heart. It is often figured flaming, or pierced, or signed with ihs. S. Augustine, S. Catharine of Siena, S. Ignatius, S. Teresa, S. Francis of Sales, among others, are so represented.

A HORN.—S. Cornelius, S. Hubert, and S. Oswald all bear horns, the two latter as hunters.

A HORSE.—S. Martin, S. George, S. Leo, and S. Emilian, are shown on horseback. S. Anastasius, S. Orestes, and S. Hippolytus are shown dragged by them to death.

THE HOST is often shown, either in the hands or over the heads of saints. Of these, S. Bernard is the only well known. S. Yvo holds a *flaming* host.

IDOLS shattered at the feet mark the victory of the saint's preaching, as with S. Philip, S. Wilfrid, or S. George.

KEYS.—The keys of the kingdom of heaven, one, two, or three, are the (emblematic) prerogative of S. Peter; but S. James the Great, according to *Cahir*, holds the keys also; and many saints do so, but clearly not in the same sense. Often the keys are those of a particular building ruled by the saint, as with S. Hubert, S. Sidwell, S. Bruno, S. Dominic, or S. Egwin.

A KNIFE is always the sign of martyrdom. S. Bartholomew, S. Ebb, S. Peter Martyr, and S. Agatha bear the weapons that sent them hence to Paradise.

A LADDER shows, as in Jacob's case, the upward path. The following saints are shown with it: S. Olave, S. Perpetua, (with a dragon at the foot); S. Leonard holds a youth by a chain, who mounts the ladder.

A LAMB (or *the* Lamb) is borne by S. John Baptist, S. Agnes, S. Genevieve, and S. Catharine. In the first case the symbolism is obvious; in the second it is surely but a *rebus;* in the other two cases a sign of innocence.

A LILY is the sign of virginity. It is held in the hands of S. Joseph, S. Dominic, S. Gabriel, S. Anthony of Padua, S. Vincent Ferrers, S. Sebastian, S. Clare, and others; while S. Angelus is shown with lilies and roses issuing from his mouth.

A LION, the royal beast, is, I believe, mostly the sign of valour. S. Jerome and S. Mark, S. Thecla, S. Prisca, and S. Dorothy are all shown with lions; but some are shown killed and torn by them, as S. Ignatius, S. Venantius, and S. Agapetus.

A MILLSTONE "cast into the sea," is the death sign of S. Aurea, S. Callixtus, S. Quirinus, and S. Victor. S. Vincent is also shown *leaning* on one, though he died a different death.

MONEY is the emblem of S. Philip, S. Matthew, and S. Martin.

NAILS.—S. Julian, S. Severus, S. Dionysius of Ephesus, and S. Pantaleon all bear these in their heads. S. Louis carries three in his hand; S. William of Norwich, three in his head and right hand; S. Alexander (pope and martyr) is nailed all over.

PALM, the martyr's sceptre, is generally borne in conjunction with other and more individual signs. S. John the Evangelist holds a palm and a cup; S. Stephen a palm and stones; S. Catharine a palm and a book; S. Angelus a palm encircled with three crowns, and so on.

A PEN is held by the evangelists and doctors of the Church.

PILGRIM STAFF.—Among those who bear this sign, the chief are: S. James Major, S. Raphael, S. Roch, and S. Sebald.

PILLARS stand behind S. Athanasius; pillars of light appear also with S. Cuthbert and S. Ephrem. S. Symeon Stylites is, of course, shown with his pillar.

A PLOUGH is the emblem of S. Richard, S. Kentigern, and S. Isidore of Madrid.

A REMONSTRANCE is carried by S. Norbert, S. Thomas Aquinas, S. Monica, and S. Clara.

A RING, the emblem, one may suppose, of being wedded to CHRIST (or His Church). In this sense it is worn by S. Barbara, S. Catharine, S. Theodora, S. Edward, and S. Edmund the bishop.

ROSES are seldom, perhaps, used with special meaning, beyond that of any other flowers, though S. Elizabeth, S. "Rose" of Lima, and S. Barbara, not to mention S. "Rosalia," are shown with garlands or bunches of those flowers in preference to others.

THE SCEPTRE is the badge of authority, and as such is borne by angels, and, among men, only by *royal* persons: S. Oswald, S. Edward, S. Louis, S. Margaret of Scotland, and so forth.

A SCOURGE is the sign of self-discipline and voluntary penance. The saints who carry this emblem are: S. Ambrose, S. Boniface, S. Alexandra, S. Symeon, S. Peter Damian, S. Guthlac, S. Eleutherius, and S. Gervase; while those whose sufferings were not self-inflicted are: S. Agapetus, S. Urban, and S. Leontius.

A SCYTHE is the emblem, by a mere play of words, given to S. Sidwell or Scythwella. It is also borne by S. Valentius, S. Walstan, and one or two other saints.

A SERPENT, "that old serpent the devil," is sometimes figured by the emblem, but oftener, I fancy, the snakes mean real snakes, or they are symbols of the machinations of any enemies. S. Hilary, S. Patrick, and S. Hilda are all supposed to have banished actual serpents; but of. S. Thecla, S. Euphemia, S. Paternus, and S. Phocas, I know no certain reason for the representation.

A SHIELD, marked with the MR, is one of the emblems of S. Gabriel; S. Michael bears one with the sun; charged with three lilies it belongs to SS. Faustinus and Simplicius; with a cross it is the emblem of S. Gengulph.

A SHIP indicates usually some miracle of calming a storm, as in the case of S. Nicholas, or S. Peter, Thomas the Carmelite, or S. Castor. S. Ursula has a ship, because of her voyage. S. Jude bears the ship as the sign of his trade. S. Anselm also is shown with a ship in his hand.

A SIEVE is held by S. Benedict, S. Hippolytus, and S. Amelberga.

A SKULL.—S. Jerome and S. Mary Magdalene bear the skull as the sign of penitence; failing any other more pointed reason, this is the meaning of it, if shown with any recluse or ascetic; but S. Eutropius bears it cloven with a sword, and S. Nicasius carries one mitred.

A STAFF is the sign of pilgrimage. Foremost among the pilgrim saints is Joseph of Arimathaea. S. James, who journeyed to Spain, S. Anthony, S. Francis Xavier, and S. Gregory Thaumaturgus also bear it.

A STAG either shows the fact that the saint was a hunter, as S. Hubert, or it is the sign of gentleness, as in the case of S. Giles, S. Conrad, or S. Macrina.

A STAR indicates divine illumination, e.g., S. Dominic, S. Bruno, S. Thomas Aquinas.

THE STIGMATA are reported to have been borne by S. Francis of Assisi, S. Catharine of Sienna, S. Margaret of Hungary, and S. Bridget. One would have expected to see them associated with S. Paul, " who bore in his body the marks of the LORD JESUS," but this is not the case.

STONES generally show the mode of martyrdom. S. Stephen, S. Timothy, S. Pancras, S. Barnabas, and S. Alphege hold them, therefore, either in their hands or vestments, or on a book. S. Jerome, on the contrary, has a stone as an instrument of penance.

THE SUN is the sign of divine love and fervour. S. Thomas Aquinas, S. Valentine, S. Nicholas of Tolentium, S. Vincent Ferrer, and S. Alban are the saints so glorified. Sunbeams play a part in the more fanciful miracles of many

G

saints, who are shown hanging their clothes on them! Among others may be mentioned S. Gothard, S. Leonorus, S. Bridget, S. David, and S. Cunegunda.

THE SWORD, like the dagger, is a token of the death endured by the saint. The following list, though not complete, may serve: S. Paul, S. James Minor, S. Valentine, S. Alban, S. John Baptist, S. Thomas à Becket, S. Peter Martyr, S. Matthias, S. Boniface, S. Maurice, S. Catharine, S. Agnes, S. Lucy, S. Pancras, S. Faith, and S. Kilian.

THORNS.—The crown of thorns shows sufferings, but thorns extracted from the feet of beasts refer to such acts performed by the saints, as with S. Jerome, S. Mark, and S. Aventinus. S. Benedict and S. Jerome are shown also kneeling in them for penance, and S. Dominic walking over them.

A TONGUE records the barbarous torture inflicted, as on S. Romanus, S. Leger, S. Eusebius, S. Placidus, and S. Livin.

A TORCH generally is the sign of great preaching and conversion of multitudes to the faith, e.g., S. Medard, S. Blaize, S, Aidan; but sometimes it shows the martyrdom, as with S. Dorothy, S. Barbara, S. Eutropia, or S. Regina.

A TOWER is, perhaps, the sign of strength with S. Ambrose; and S. Barbara carries it in reference to her prison.

A TREE is nearly always simply the representation of an incident belonging to the life (or death) of the saint. S. Sebastian is shown tied to one, so also are S. Hippolytus, S. Amphibalus, S. Corona, S. Crispin, and others.

A TRUMPET shows the message of GOD delivered with no uncertain sound· S. Jerome and S. Vincent Ferrer are so shown.

WATER is often shown brought from a rock by the saints, e.g., S. Honoratus, S. Francis Assisi, S. Columban, and S. Ladislaus.

Others are shown walking upon it after the example of our LORD, e.g., S. Conrad, S. Juvenal, S. Aldegondes, and S. Peter Alcantara.

A WELL, as distinguished from a fountain, (q.v.) is, I think, rather a complimentary tribute of a later age to the power of a saint who was supposed to have given virtue to the waters, by his prayers.

WHEEL.—S. Catharine is not the only saint whose emblem is the wheel, nor is this wonderful, considering how common an instrument of torture and death it was in ancient times. S. Euphemia, S. Quentin, S. Donatus, and S. Eucratida have it as their sign. S. Willigis bears a shield of a wheel *arg.* on a field *gu.*, and S. Martin's arms are *gu.* a wheel *or.*

A WOLF accompanies S. Vedast and S. Blaize, because of miracles connected therewith. S. Columban kneels among them to show the hardship and desolation of his life.

CHAPTER XI.

The Ever Blessed Trinity.

"No man hath seen GOD at any time:" and no man, one would have thought, had dared to make the likeness of the Three that bear witness in heaven in the light that no man can approach unto.

Such however is not the case. The triangle or the intertwined fish, that satisfied the primitive Christians, were not considered realistic enough as time went on.

There can be no question that it was reverence, and not unbelief; reticence, and not want of skill, that hindered the chisel and the brush of the early artist from attempting to portray the unknown and the unknowable.

Would that the same reverence and godly fear had prevailed until the present day, as for eight centuries at least it did.

Up till that time, though the Trinity was often *shown* it was not *presented*.

The course of progress was somewhat in this order:

First, the figure of the God-Man is represented accompanied by the Dove; a Hand above shows the Almighty FATHER.

Or, the Lamb and the Cross, the Hand and the Dove; but these three are seldom all united, or closely joined in one composition.

Next, as in the Basilicas of the fifth, sixth, and seventh centuries, CHRIST, the Lamb, the Dove, and the FATHER'S Hand are always shown together.

S. Dunstan is perhaps the first *name* associated in an entirely anthropomorphic showing of the Trinity. He left behind him a MS. in which the FATHER and the SON are shown of equal age and stature, while the HOLY GHOST is represented as a youth.

He was not, however, the first or only one, even in the ninth century, to draw such pictures. The FATHER, and the SON, with the Dove between them; three equal human figures with the Dove over the Head of one; the FATHER distinguished by a Tiara, the SON bearing a Cross; three equal figures totally undistinguishable; in such ways did men dare to "climb up into heaven."

It is enough to refer my readers to the pages of Didron's *Iconography* for a fuller account of the origin and progress of such picturing. I will content myself with very few actual illustrations of this sacred subject.

Fig. A. is dogmatic, reverent, and in every sense unobjectionable. From unity as the centre, Trinity springs, yet the centre of unity is only found by the conjunction of the Trinity. Didron gives this as from a French Miniature of the thirteenth century.

On Plate XV., fig. 1, is shown an early example from the Catacombs.

Figs. 2 and 3 need no reference save the word *passim*.

Fig. 4. the early Christian symbol of the three fish.

Fig. 5 is from a French Missal of the twelfth century, and I have given it because it is the type of several existing examples in our own country. Unfortunately I have lost a very beautiful brass-rubbing from a Derbyshire Church, which shows the same subject far better treated.

Fig. 6, from a French book of the Hours, published 1524, is perhaps a valuable example, as it shows at the same time the anthropomorphic attempt to show three faces or *personas* in one, and also shows the shield of the Trinity of which I give two other specimens.

The first, fig. 8, is the typical one. The second, fig. 9, drawn from glass in Dunmow Church, is noteworthy, as lacking the words *Non est*. I do not suppose the artist was in any way guilty of conscious heresy, but why he omitted the usual confession is a matter of wonder.

It is stated by some that this shield of the Trinity is *never* found in England, save in the eastern counties, or at least where distinctly French influence affected the county.

This may be so generally, and I am not able to recall any specimens, save in Essex, Suffolk, Norfolk, or Kent; but Husenbeth gives *one* example at least from Crossthwaite, in Cumberland. The Heraldic description of fig. 8 is as follows: *Gu.* an orle and pall, *arg.* conjoined and surmounted of four plates at the dexter and sinister chief, the base and the fesse points respectively. The first, inscribed **Pater**; the second, **Filius**; and the third, **Spiritus Sanctus**; the centre, **Deus**; the connecting portions of the orle between them having **non est**; and those of the pall, **est**.

Other examples differ in their tincture, or the contractions employed, or the writing of the name of the third Person, which is sometimes **S. S.** or **spus sctus**, sometimes **spus** alone.

In Vincent's MSS. in the College of Arms, a shield belonging to Christ Church Priory is given with the field *az.* the rest as above; and in Blythborough Church, a window has the field *az.* and the Trinity *or*.

Fig. 7 shows a representation of the Trinity at the Creation of Eve.

And Fig. 10, the sixteenth century device which most of us have often seen in our childhood painted on the commandment boards, or carved or gilded on the pulpit or its sounding-board.

Of the Persons separately.

(DISTINCT FROM THE TRINITY AS SUCH.)

Until the fourteenth century, at any rate, it is by no means easy to speak definitely, as though sometimes the age points to the "ancient of days," this is not universally true ; nor can anything be said to show whether we are contemplating a figure of the Almighty FATHER, the Divine SON, or the HOLY SPIRIT. But from the above mentioned date and onwards, GOD the FATHER was always shown as an old man, generally crowned as a King (or Emperor) until the fifteenth century, when the Papal Tiara * replaced the Regal Crown.

The Renaissance, with its inevitable Paganism, reverted to a conception almost indistinguishable from the Olympian " Father of the Gods."

The HOLY SPIRIT was more rarely shown separately from a "Trinity" than the Almighty FATHER, and the explanation is not far to seek. Since Divine Revelation has "given us a sign" men had no need to cast about for means to show the Comforter to their fellows.

In the form of a dove S. John the Baptist recognised the presence of the HOLY GHOST abiding upon the SAVIOUR, wherefore from the dawn of Christianity until to-day this has been the almost universal method of portrayal.

An example is given on Plate XV., fig. 11, which gives the common type of this emblem.

Very often, however, the Holy Dove became seven, in reference to the "seven Spirits of GOD," † and to the seven gifts of the HOLY GHOST. These doves were shown, either surrounding the head of our Blessed LORD, or that of our Lady when holding Him in her arms. This implies no undue mariolatry when we remember the words of the heavenly message : " The HOLY GHOST shall come upon thee, and the power of the Highest shall overshadow thee."‡

These gifts, as enumerated by the prophet Isaiah, are Sapientia, Intellectus, Consilium, Fortitudo, Scientia, Pietas, Timor. They *correspond*, though they do not *coincide* with the qualities ascribed to the glorified LORD in the Apocalypse : " Power and riches and wisdom and strength and honour and glory and blessing." Sometimes the seven Doves carry or stand on scrolls inscribed with the names of the gifts, sometimes they are shown alone. Occa-

---

* True, the artists often tried to exalt the Almighty a little above the Pope by crowning the Tiara five times instead of thrice, but nothing could redeem their efforts from the bonds of Papal idolatry too sad for words.

† Rev. v. 6.   ‡ S. Luke i. 35.

sionally the doves are *six* in number, as in a window of the twelfth century in Chartres Cathedral, given by Didron, Vol. i. p. 486.

Perhaps the most remarkable example of a dove* is that shown in Twining's *Emblems*, as appropriated to Elisha. Here the reference is obviously to the double portion of the spirit. Many of the Saints, Doctors, and Fathers of the Church are shown with the Holy Dove perched upon the shoulder and whispering the "hidden wisdom" into their ear—

Tu septiformis munere
Dextrae Dei tu digitus
Tu rite promissum patris
Sermone ditans guttura.

This inspiration, given almost unsought, as by the passing of a bird, is in harmony with our LORD'S promise: "Take no thought, it shall be given what ye shall speak."

Another emblem of the HOLY GHOST is the Flame of Pentecost. Fig. 3, Plate XXVIII., is copied from the Robe of the Order of the HOLY GHOST, preserved in the Cluny Museum. Of the Eagles given in Twining's *Emblems*, I am not at all sure whether the bird of Elisha is an eagle (I prefer to call it a dove), nor of the undoubted eagle, whether it has any relation to the HOLY SPIRIT.

Concerning the portrayal of our Blessed LORD, something is said in Chapter XIII., but it belongs to this Chapter to speak of the subject generally, and as apart from the more emblematical representations.

In so far as purely human pictures are in question, there is naturally no prohibition or limitation whatever of liberty to depict the Son of Man. Nor is there any occasion to describe the methods and modes of representation.

From the cradle to the Ascension at least, all such pictures are naturalistic, traditionally historic, records of His life on earth.

When He is shown in glory, or figured with the seven candles, the rainbow, the sword, and so forth, the Apocalypse is the authority for such pictures, and it is sufficient.

When the picture is theological, as in a Trinity, still there is no breach of Reverence and Godly Fear, *if* the other sacred persons are not anthropomorphic.

Possibly my readers will disagree with me when I say of the accompanying illustration,† in spite of its crude and childish realism (or rather falseness), that it comes nearer than any other such effort, to success in teaching Truth. Con- sider it for a moment, apart from all preconception of right or wrong in picturing the Godhead, and does not the infinite pathos of it come home to one's heart?

* Or Eagle? † From a French miniature of the fourteenth century (Didron).

"He being in the Form of GOD . . . made Himself of no reputation," or (as the Greek has it) ἐκένωσεν ἑαυτὸν, "he emptied or *stripped Himself*," and so divested of all majesty, receiving from His FATHER merely the pilgrim's outfit for His travel, He took His journey to seek and to save His brethren.

What shall we say of our LORD as Orpheus, because "never man spake like this man?" Yet this was by no means an unfavoured notion by the earliest followers of CHRIST.

Of the Good Shepherd one need say nothing here, since this and other emblems are dealt with in a later chapter.

CHAPTER XII.

The Holy Name.

SINCE the Name of our Salvation is not only that which is above every name, but also declared in Holy Writ to be the one at which (or in which) every knee should bow, it is only natural that our LORD'S most Blessed Name should figure frequently in sacred art. Moreover, in the earliest ages, when such art was in its infancy, the simplest signs would naturally be the ones most commonly employed. The Catacombs of Rome provide us with an almost infinite supply of examples, if we wish to see how the Name was written upon the resting-places of those who slept in Him. And as the first altars were generally above the graves of those who had laid down their lives for Him who had given life to them, so the earliest existing examples of sacred art are to be found in funereal inscriptions, and memorials of the faithful departed.

There are, as we all know, two names belonging to our Divine Redeemer; the one official, the other personal; CHRIST—JESUS. Of these the former is far more frequently found in the first ages. Nor can we wonder at this, since it was some time before the name of JESUS* was the sole prerogative of the King of the Jews. There were many called JESUS, but *One* CHRIST. To the early Christians JESUS was *Christ*, and the Christian mourners loved to write the beloved Name of Hope above the bed of the sleeping Christian.

But we must remember that both names are Greek, and to understand the symbols as we see them, we must see how they came to be written as they are.

In old uncial letters the names would read thus: IHCOYC—XPICTOC; that is to say that the *sigma*, which we nowadays generally print Σ, was not then so written, but almost exactly like a modern C. These names, like many other words, were contracted, and would usually be written with only two or three of their letters: therefore the names would read IH—XP if the two first letters were employed, or IHC—  XPC, if the two first and final were used, or often IC—XC, the final and last, would serve.

As time went on, and the Latin element of Christianity gradually outweighed the Greek, the name of our LORD was written in very strange fashion. Many ancient coins show the course of transition. The above illustration from a

---

* JESUS called Justus was doubtless only one of many Jewish converts owning the same name as our Redeemer (Col. iv. 11).

coin of John I. is remarkable, as many of the letters seem of interchangeable value, while Λ = L in one place, L is L in another; the U in one place is the Greek Υ, and in another the Latin. The spelling is neither Greek nor Latin, but a mixture of the two.

The ordinary symbol of our LORD'S name was for centuries however the XP, the sign vouchsafed to Constantine in the heavenly vision with the promise, *sub hoc signo vinces.**

Of this a few variant examples are shown, but they might be multiplied a hundred-fold. There is only one to be specially noticed which shows the letter N for "Nazarene" in conjunction with the X and P.

Didron, I regret to notice, says that the N is most probably for *Noster*, and that the monogram reads Christus Noster—not quite a common phrase. One almost wonders that he did not say it was P.N., *Pater Noster!*

Another ancient example figured by the same author is interesting, as showing the Greek letters adopted in clearly Roman. Yet the A attempt to Latinise. The ser- mystic signification to the solution.

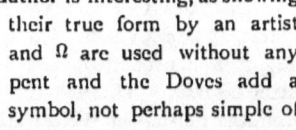

their true form by an artist and Ω are used without any pent and the Doves add a symbol, not perhaps simple of

The H which is E, the C which is S, and the P which is R, would not unnaturally be a source of error to transcribers who were not always competent translators; and so it came to pass, partly, no doubt, from carelessness, partly from ignorance, and partly, perchance, from scrupulosity, the H and the C were kept by the Latins and the mediaevalists in the Name of JESUS, as the P in CHRIST; so IHC. and XPC. were kept until, in course of time, when first the Lombardic, and then the black letter displaced the Roman type, the names were written, 𝔦𝔥𝔠 and 𝔵𝔭𝔠. Though, for one example of the latter, there are a thousand of the former.

But it was not always 𝔦𝔥𝔠 that was written, for clearly there were not wanting those who knew that the C was really S, so they wrote 𝔦𝔥𝔰 and 𝔵𝔭𝔰. But what of the 𝔥? This was, I think, never understood in the middle ages to equal 𝔢, and therefore it was regarded as part of the name 𝔦𝔥𝔢𝔰𝔲𝔰. This is the more readily understood when we remember how many names in which the letter J is concerned were spelt in Latin, with the addition or substitution of H, as 𝔥𝔦𝔢𝔯𝔲𝔰𝔞𝔩𝔢𝔪, or

---

* Eusebius gives the following account of the *Labarum* of Constantine :—" In the year 311, when about to march against Maxentius, he prayed earnestly to God for guidance; whereupon, in the noonday sky, above the sun there appeared a cross of light, with the words, Τουτῳ Νικα. The following day, after pondering in his mind what manner of vision this might be, he caused skilful embroiderers and craftsmen to make a banner bearing this sign, under which his army marched to victory."

hieronymus.* Accordingly, the Name JESUS was oftener written with the H than without it. And not merely in Latin, for I have often seen it so spelt in English and French in fifteenth and sixteenth century writings.

In ancient decoration we have sometimes the vocative ihesu contracted to ihu. Sometimes the nominative ihus, ihs, or ihc. Plate XVII., fig. 6, shows an unusual mediaeval contraction †S, sketched from the wall of Saint John Baptist's Church in Winchester.

I do not think there is much doubt of the history of the H. Nor has its place in the familiar Jesuit monogram anything to do with the fanciful translation accepted by some as an article of belief. The ingenious Dr. Brewer calls this the Church *Anagram*, and gravely says:

    Greek—Iησους Ημετερ Cοςωτηρ.
    Latin—Iesus Hominum Salvator.
    English—Jesus Heavenly Saviour.
    German—Jesus Heiland Seligmacher.

I think nothing need be added to this save, perchance, the little child's translation—I. Have. Suffered! †

On Plates XVI. and XVII. are collected many ancient examples of the Sacred Name. Plate XVI., fig. 1, a simple ihc from the roof of Blythborough Church. Fig. 2, from a painted panel in the ceiling of S. Alban's Abbey. Fig. 3 is from stained glass in Thaxted Church. Fig. 4 is taken from Twining's *Emblems*, as from the cloisters at Wells Cathedral. Figs. 11 and 12 are said to be from Ancient Embroidery (Parker, *Kalendar Illustrated*).

Fig. 1, Plate XVII., is from old ironwork at Gisors, in France. Fig. 2, a very remarkable example of minute detail, is from stained glass in Holy Trinity, Oxford. Fig. 4 is the monogram on the mitre of William of Wykeham. Fig. 7 is from stained glass in Much Hadham Church. Here notice a strange backsliding in the word *Super*, which is spelt without the slightest uncertainty, *Cuper*. Fig. 15, the Font at Saltwood, in Kent, gives a still more remarkable spelling to the Name—Jehiu, or possibly Jehsu. Here it is coupled (rather early, I think) with our Lady's name, Marya. Fig. 13 is a very beautiful monogram from stained glass in Stanford Church. Fig. 3 is a *very* late example, late but very healthy, from an old book in my possession. Fig. 5, from Embroidery. Fig. 8, from a carved wooden shield of the sixteenth century. This shows a lapse into "Romanism," rather before the general movement of the Renaissance in England. Figs. 9 and 10 are copied from the wonderful wall tiles surrounding the High Altar of Malvern Abbey. Figs. 11 and 12 from the wall of a Church in

---

* Note also, on the other hand, the strange anglicizing of the precious stone, the hyacinth, which in Rev. xxi. 20 is given as a "Jacinth."

† S. Bernadine of Siena is *said* to be the originator of "Jesus Hominum Salvator." And he was summoned to Rome on a charge of heresy, founded on his custom of carrying about a paper inscribed with the Monogram.

Hampshire. Fig. 14, from the Font in S. Keverne, Cornwall. Here I fancy the upper letters are alpha and omega, though the latter is a distinct M. Compare with the M of fig. 15.

The 𝔦𝔥𝔲 𝔪𝔠𝔶 of fig. 8 on Plate XVI. is from a fourteenth century Brass in Higham Ferrers Church; the IHESVS MARIA of fig. 10 from the painting of the Mass of S. Gregory. The last example figured on this plate, fig. 13, is perhaps the most remarkable monogram extant. It is taken from a carved tablet behind the High Altar of Louvain Cathedral. The whole composition shows the figure of S. John Baptist, and the donor (or deceased commemorated by the monument). The wonderfully ingenious weaving together of the Death and the Rising to Life again of our LORD is worthy of all admiration. The size of the original is about four feet by two.

In the employment of the name, or monogram, nowadays, I may just suggest that in Gothic-work we should prefer 𝔦𝔥𝔠 to 𝔦𝔥𝔰, or if we use the name in full we may or may not use the 𝔥; but in any case we should never hark back to the days of the Catacombs, and do violence to a mediaeval design by putting the Roman I.H.S., still less the quasi-Greek XP. If, on the other hand, our work is in a Classic, Renaissance, or Romanesque style, we shall only fall into the opposite extreme of error, by using the Gothic character.

The all Holy Name should, moreover, be ever used with thought and care, and never simply to pad an empty corner, or fill a void in a design.

I shall probably only echo the feelings of my readers if I add, while Jhesus-Maria is out of harmony with the universal language of Christendom, the words, " IESVS MARY JOSEPH," so often found in modern Roman work, may be written and left without comment.

Since, in the words of the legend surrounding No. 7, Plate XVII.,

hoc est nomen quod super omne nomen.

CHAPTER XIII.

Other Emblems of our Lord.

I.

THE AGNUS DEI.

IN all ways the most scriptural Emblem of the Divine Redeemer, since under this figure both in the Old and New Testaments CHRIST is preached. Yet for our present purposes one of the most difficult to employ. Adopted in the very earliest ages, constantly figured in the Catacombs, carved and painted, pictured in stone and wood and glass and needlework, for all that, with a thousand examples before us, it is hard to find a dozen that are devotional. Perhaps the best that was ever depicted is fig. 4, Plate XVIII., given in Parker's *Calendar of the English Church*, and many other books, as from an Italian sculpture of the eleventh century. It combines extreme refinement with conventionality, and yet it is unmistakably a Lamb.

Fig. 9 is from stained glass of the fourteenth century. Fig. 8 is a modified version of the Agnus Dei on the Zion cope. The original is too hideous to reproduce, and this is given as a modern version, simply representing the pose and the arrangement of the sun and moon and stars surrounding it. Fig. 7 is an early example from the Catacombs. Fig. 13 is from stained glass in Newick Church. Here the Lamb is a *Ram*. Fig. 10 shews an Italian example of the twelfth century. It is noticeable for the Patriachal Cross to which the banner is attached, as well as for the Chalice which receives the Blood of the Covenant.

The Agnus Dei is generally shown standing, though sometimes lying "as it were slain," either on an altar, or on the book with the seven seals, as in fig. 14. In all but the earliest examples, the head is surrounded with the Nimbus of Divinity. In mediaeval times the cross and banner of the Resurrection was carried.

Sometimes the Lamb is shown standing on the Mount of GOD, from whence flow the four streams, typifying the water of life dispensed by the four Evangelists.

Other representations may be noticed without reproduction. They are such as show the Lamb of GOD with seven horns, which is inelegant, and with seven *eyes*, which is painful.

It was almost inevitable that such things should be attempted, but one cannot but regret the striving after literalism, since, in spite of faithful endeavour, the impossible remains where it was—beyond man's understanding.

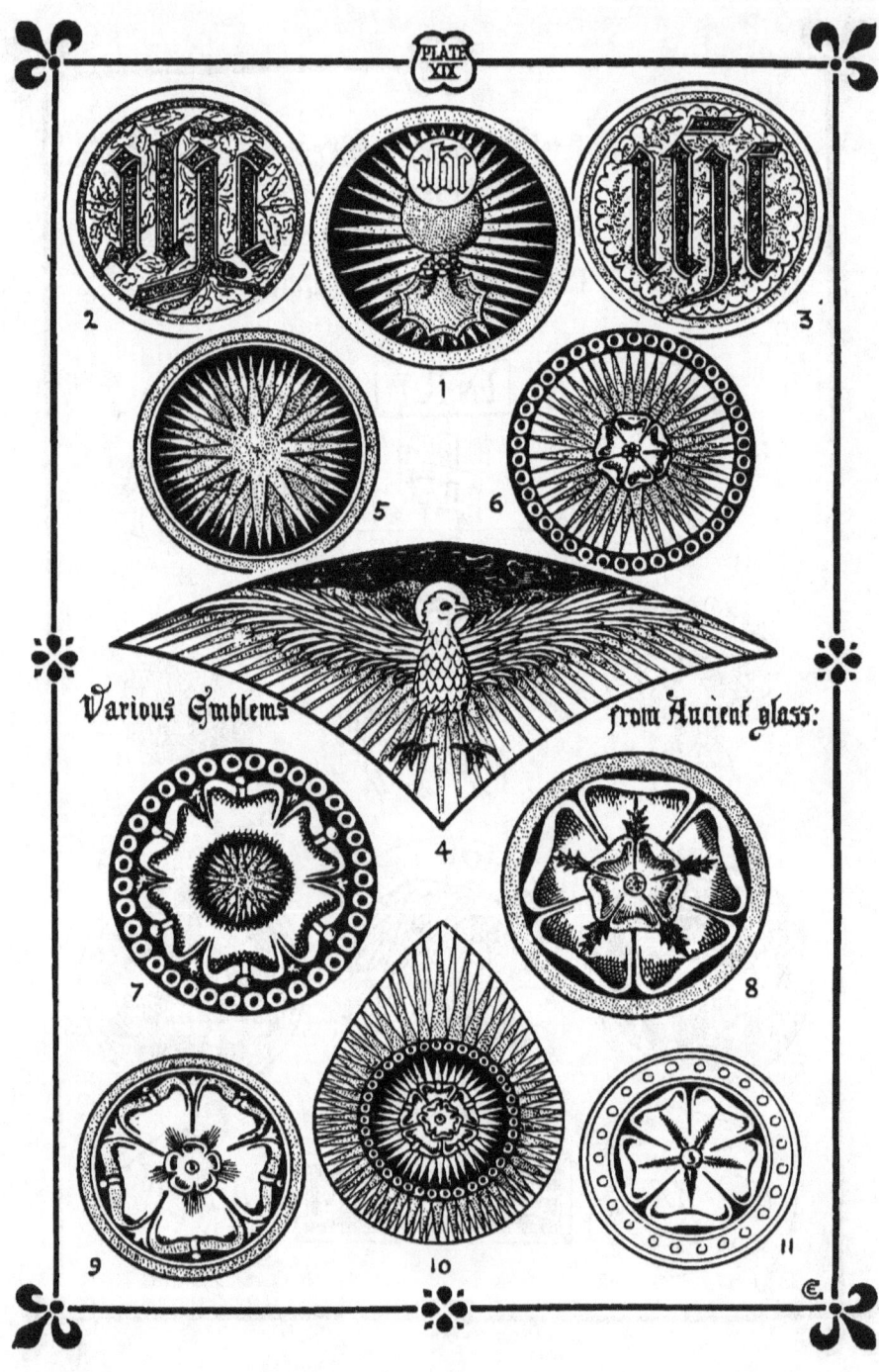

II.

THE ALPHA AND OMEGA.

The first and last letter of the Greek alphabet are constantly to be found in conjunction with the Cross of CHRIST, as with the monogram of His most Holy Name, as may be seen from the two examples here given, both of which are from early Christian monuments. The examples of mediaeval type are few and far between,  and I think it is better now to write the *words* alpha and omega on scrolls, rather than to try and gothicise Greek characters, which however carefully done, leaves them almost unrecognisable.

III.

THE ANCHOR.

The emblem of Hope: as says the writer to the Hebrews—"Which we have as an anchor of the soul, both sure and stedfast."

This emblem fell more or less into disuse after the earliest ages, when, as may be seen, the anchor combined itself with the cross, which indeed is itself our Hope, and consequently our anchor. (See Plate XX., figs. 3 and 4.)

That it re-appeared, and was frequently used in the middle ages, does not quite establish its claim to identity. It may be when we find it carved on stone or wood in an old Church, the anchor of S. Nicholas, S. Clement, or S. Felix, of whom the two first Saints are among the most popular of our Patrons.

Nor do I think that the anchor, the heart, and the cross were ever generally intended to figure the theological virtues, or as they are called in slipshod terminology, the "three graces."

If this were the case, we should find the three *together*, since all three "remain;" but I never so saw them—off a book-marker.

It would appear safer to conclude that as CHRIST *is* our Hope, and as Hope is called the anchor, it is a perfectly legitimate emblem to employ as *His* sign, rather than *our* sign, which it really comes to when we think it out. On Plate XXIX., fig. 31, there is an ancient example from a bench end, and there is another just like it (but reversed) in Abbotsham Church; but as the companion shields bear cobbler's tools, compasses, and squares, oak leaves, pewter pots, and all manner of trade implements, no certain evidence is afforded as to its meaning.

IV.

THE CROSS.

"Among the first Christians, the Instrument of GOD'S Suffering and man's redemption, the Cross, was made the chief emblem of their faith, the chief mark of their community, their standard and their watchword."

So says Hope in his *Historical Essay on Architecture*; but Didron goes somewhat further when he writes: "The Cross is more than a mere figure of CHRIST; it is CHRIST Himself, or His Symbol."*

Hence it is that a pious feeling, however misguided, led men to invent a history and a pedigree of the Very Rood on which depended our salvation.

The seeds from the Tree of Life, planted by Seth in his father's grave, grew into three shoots united in a single trunk. Hence came Moses' Rod. Hence Solomon cut a beam for his palace, which was incapable of use for secular purposes, since, like the bed of Procrustes, it was always either too short or too long for its intended position.

Thrown into the pool of Bethesda, it gave the wondrous virtues to its waters. The wood being providentially discovered, when required for the greater Healing of the Nations, was fashioned for use on Calvary. Buried by the Jews, it was exhumed by S. Helen, and exalted for the adoration of the faithful.

This history may be conveniently read in the *Legendary History of the Cross*, by John Ashton (T. F. Unwin). It is not worth detailed repetition here, nor would it be apposite to our present purpose to mention the subsidiary characters introduced, Heraclius and Chrosoes, Maximilla and the rest. Suffice it to say that the impress of this legend is left imprinted even in our English Prayer Book, the calendar of which contains two days—the Invention, May 3rd, and the Exaltation, September 14th.

Its impress on the world and on the Church is deep and ineradicable.

Santa Croce, Santa Cruz, S. Cross, Vera Cruz, and Holyrood will stand as long as the world endures. The Sign of the Cross, the sacred mark, will last until the same sign of the Son of Man appears in the heavens. And while we can only wonder at the credulity that could accept as historical the "History" of the Cross, we may fairly accord to that history its value, in fixing the sign and perpetuating its pious veneration by the faithful, and not merely a credulous and superstitious adoration to be abhorred of all faithful men.

The original form of the Cross is uncertain. Some vigorously assert that the Rood was a T, the Tau Cross of S. Anthony. Others go further, and declare that it was not a "cross" at all, and that neither the *Crux* of the Romans, nor the σταυρος of the Greeks implied a crossbar. To both these assertions it is perhaps sufficient to reply that a dictionary is not an effective enough weapon to destroy the tradition of 1,800 years.

Nor is the pre-Christian use of the Tau Cross of any great weight, especially as heathen examples of many sorts of crosses, dating back to the remotest antiquity, are equally at our disposal. Tiglath Pileser is shown with the cross, fylfot ⊞; and the ancient worship of Central America and Mexico included the veneration of this sign. The Tau Cross is found on Monuments at Palenque and elsewhere; the Greek Cross ✠ in Central America (as well as in Egypt!).

---

* *Iconography*, Vol. i., p. 367 (Bohn).

Volumes might be written, and have been, to attempt the solution of this fact that the Cross has a venerable past, as it has a noble present, and a still more majestic future.

Tradition says that the wood of Isaac's burden was in the form of a Cross. It is so represented in many early pictures, and some commentators on the sacred text go so far as to say that it was the sight of this shape that moved the merciful heart of the everlasting FATHER to stay the hand of Abraham.

So, too, the blood upon the doorposts of the Israelites is supposed to have been marked cross wise, and (with far greater probability) it is said that the serpent in the wilderness was lifted up upon a cross. This not only appeals to our reason because it would be the aptest shape to hold it, but it also fits our LORD'S own words, *As* that was, *so* should the Son of Man be lifted up. This "Cross" is sometimes represented as a T, and sometimes as a Latin cross. The words of Ezekiel ix. 4,—"Set a *mark* upon the foreheads of the men that sigh for the abominations"—are rendered in the Vulgate.* *Signa Tau super frontes virorum.*

A much more obscure reference to the Cross is discovered by some in Genesis xlvii. 31, when Jacob worshipped *conversus ad lectuli caput*, which stands in the LXX., Jacob worshipped ἐπὶ τὸ ἄκρον τῆς ῥάβδου αὐτοῦ. Hence it is supposed that the Patriarch's benediction was given with his crutched staff upraised, while Joseph "sware unto him" by the Holy Sign.

Be these things as they may, there is something to be said for Didron's name which he applies to the T, as the anticipatory cross, the foreshadowing of the complete sign of the Son of Man as we know it.

Yet, when we have to draw a cross, in a heraldic or emblematic sense of the word, we must first ask what sort of a cross, since there are some forty varieties, without attempting to count the innumerable floriated and ornamented designs wherewith men have delighted to honour the mark of their high calling.

On Plate XX. will be found forty-one crosses, in which all the leading forms are represented.

Fig. 1. The LATIN CROSS, called also the Cross of the Passion, with three short members and one long. These three shorter arms are usually equal, but sometimes the upright is longer, and sometimes much shorter than the horizontal limbs.

Fig. 2. The CALVARY CROSS is the same cross placed upon steps, which steps are sometimes named and inscribed—*Fides*
Spes
Caritas.

Figs. 3 and 4 are two early examples of the ANCHOR CROSS.

---

* Deane in the *Worship of the Serpent* not only dwells upon this and other Old Testament allusions, but he shows with some reason, that our LORD'S most puzzling words, "Let a man *take up his cross*," may here find explanation. "Let a man *mark* himself as My disciple, with the old sign of Salvation."

Fig. 16. The GREEK CROSS, has all its arms of equal length.

Figs. 11, 12, 13. The TAU, or Crutched Cross, of which mention has been made above.

Fig. 5 is the PATRIARCHAL CROSS, borne by Patriarchs and Popes. This has two cross-bars.

Fig. 6 is however the form which the PAPAL CROSS assumed in later times, with three cross-bars.

Figs. 7 and 8. The CROSS PATÉE.

Figs. 9 and 10. The MALTESE CROSS, as worn by the Knights Templars and the Knights of S. John.

Figs. 14 and 29 are two varieties of the FYLFOT. These are in Heraldic language said to be the rebated form of

Fig. 28. The CROSS POTENT.
Fig. 18. The CROSS FLEURIE.
Fig. 21. The CROSS FLEURETTÉE.
Fig. 19. The CROSS PATONCE.
Fig. 20. The CROSS MOLINE.
Fig. 26. The CROSS BOTONNÉE, or trefoiled.
Fig. 27. The CROSS POMMÉE.
Fig. 32. The CROSS CROSSLET.
Fig. 31. The CROSS URDÉE.
Fig. 33. The CROSS FITCHÉE.
Fig. 30. The CROSS FOURCHÉE.
Fig. 34. The CROSS RECERCELÉE.
Fig. 35. The CROSS POINTED.
Fig. 24. The CROSS QUADRATE.

Fig. 25. The Cross SALTIRE, familiar to us all as the Cross of S. Andrew, S. Alban, and S. Patrick.

Fig. 15. The Cross QUARTER PIERCED.
Fig. 17. The Cross QUARTERLY PIERCED.

Fig. 37 is the CROSS OF IONA, the terribly vulgarised cross of the public cemetery.

Figs. 38, 39, 40, and 41 are various early examples from the Catacombs and elsewhere. A few others will be found in Chapter XII., p. 90, "On our LORD'S Name."

Any Cross may be made with the various Heraldic border lines (see Chapter XXI.).

So, for example, fig. 22 is a CROSS ENGRAILED; fig. 23 is a CROSS RAGULÉE; fig. 36 is a CROSS WAVY. So, too, a Cross may be bordered with a line, in which case it is said to be fimbriated. Any "charge" or figure may be shown crosswise four; crosses, stars, roses, or *fleur de lys*, etc., etc. Any cross may be fitchée or spiked at the bottom limb, so that fig. 34 or 26, if treated like fig. 33, would be described respectively as a Cross recercelée fitchée, or botonnée fitchée.

A few additional varieties of the heraldic cross are drawn on Plate XXI.
(1) The *Cross Portate*, i.e., the cross as it would be borne by our blessed LORD on the *Via dolorosa*.
(2) The *Cross Pommettée*.
(3) The *Cross Barbée*.
(4) The *Cross double fitchée*.
(5) The *16-point Cross*.
(6) The *Cross Moussue*.
(7) The *Paternoster Cross*, formed by a string of beads.
(8) The *Interlaced Cross*.
(9) The *Double Parted Cross*.
(10) The *Cross of S. James*, so called because it is borne by the Knights of S. Iago in Spain.
(11) The *Cross Crescented*.
(12) The *Cross Degraded*.
(13) The *Cross Triparted*.
(14) The *Cross Corded*.
(15) The *Cross Clechée*.
(16) The *Cross Entrailed* (always blazoned *sable*).

The Cross of S. Lazarus is—on a field *arg.* an eight-pointed cross *vert*, borne by the Knights of S. Lazarus.

A cross is said to be *engoulée* when its ends enter the mouths of lions or leopards. It is called *Gringollée* when from its extremities issue serpents' heads.

I fear to go further in this direction, lest too wide a field of blasonry be opened out; but it is perhaps as well to have described the Cross at some length, in order that when it is used in decoration it may be advisedly and soberly used with a due sense of the meaning of the "sign of so great a thing."

> Crux fidelis, inter omnes
> Arbor una nobilis:
> Nulla talem silva profert
> Fronde flore germine:
> Dulce signum, dulce ferrum
> Dulce pondus sustinens.

V.

THE CANDLESTICK.

This emblem is of frequent occurrence in early Christian monuments, but it soon dropped out of use, and was practically unknown in the middle ages. There is one curious example in Twining's *Christian Symbols and Emblems* which is given in that book as from the Catacombs (Plate XIV., fig. 1).

Its chief point of interest lies in the base, which is supported on four feet, one human, one of an eagle, another of an ox, and the last of a lion.

It is certainly worthy of remark, while CHRIST is the Light of the World, and, on all hands, a candle or lamp is acknowledged to show this truth, that the lamp or candlestick is not oftener found depicted. Possibly the candles on the altars of our Churches were supposed to present a sufficient object-lesson—"The signification that CHRIST is the very true Light of the World," was not an invented symbolism of Edward VI.'s Injunction in 1547, but expressed the universal faith of all the ages.

I. H. Hazé, in his *Brevis Explicatio*, says, "The candlesticks crown the altar .... to figure CHRIST our LORD, Who is the Light of the World, and as it were a Heavenly Torch sending fire on the earth that it may be kindled."

The seven-branched form in which the candelabrum appeared is clearly traceable to the sevenfold lamp of the Tabernacle and the Temple, and to the seven golden candlesticks of the Apocalypse, in the midst of which stood the Son of Man, with His countenance as the sun "shining in its strength." *

The candlestick of the Temple, as shown on the Arch of Titus, is doubtless a fairly accurate record of the light of the old Sanctuary, profanely quenched by Gentile hands.

VI.

THE FISH.

This may be, perhaps, more truly called a *Rebus* than an Emblem, in its first inception at least. Fishers of men regarded them as fish, of course; but I doubt not that to some pious scribe who had written these first four words, Ἰησοῦς Χριστὸς Θεοῦ Υἱός, it suddenly occurred that the initials suggested Ἰχθύς, and only needed the Σ; so Σωτήρ was added, and the sacred *Rebus* was formed, by what men call an accident.

Fig. 16, Plate XVIII., is an early signet ring, bearing the initials and the figure of a fish impaled by an anchor. There can be no doubt of the direct reference to our LORD here, and though many antiquaries † have laboured to prove the 1,000 examples in the Catacombs to be merely "trade marks," I think scarce any reasonable being will doubt that they are religious tokens, and if not referring to CHRIST Himself, refer to *Christians;* for, as Tertullian says, *Nos pisciculi secundum* ἰχθὺν *nostrum in aquâ nascimur.*

* Rev. i. 16.

† Didron (*Iconography*, Vol. i. p. 356), with a marble sarcophagus before him, which shows a shepherd carrying a lamb with others at his feet, a fish and an anchor, flanking the composition; goes to the pains of giving an epitome of the life of the poor inmate, "He was doubtless a fisherman who afterwards became an opulent breeder of sheep."—*Credat Iudaeus.*

Other Emblems of our Lord.

The Fish Bladder, the *Vesica Piscis* () is undoubtedly a mere architectural version of the Fish, and is so distinctly a religious figure that its use is forbidden, by common consent, to any person or corporation other than ecclesiastic, either for seal or ring or shield of arms.

Many old Fonts of Norman date bear fishes, sometimes singly, sometimes in groups, sometimes Mermen—half man, half fish—as on the ancient font in S. Peter's, Cambridge.

In Braybrook Church there is a human headed fish devouring a natural one. I suppose this indicates our life by feeding on our IΧΘΥC. Both these fonts are very early, and I know of no other or later examples. Figs. 15 and 17 on Plate XVIII. are purely armorial fish from a Belgian Brass. Fig. 6 from the border of a window in Kingsdown Church.

The three interlaced fishes on Plate XV. I regard, rightly or wrongly, as more likely to symbolize the Holy Trinity, or Baptism in His Name, than CHRIST Himself. See also Plate XXIII., fig. 8, from the Font of S. Gulval, Cornwall, where the three fish are placed next the Cross on the same shield.

VII.
THE HAND.

Here, again, we are far from certain whether this Hand is the *Dextera Domini*, or the Hand of the LORD CHRIST, whose own Right Hand and Holy Arm got Him the victory. On Plate XXIV. will be found three specimens. Fig. 8, from a Brass dated 1400, at Nordhausen, is the more noteworthy, because it has a distinct *Triune* nimbus. Fig. 7 shows, I fancy, rather the victory of CHRIST risen above the *clouds* and *crowned* with glory. Fig. 9 I drew many years ago at Worcester, from a paten taken from the Tomb of Bishop Walter de Cantelupe, A.D. 1236. Here the nimbus is cruciform, and may, or may not, refer to our LORD. Fig. 11 is from the seal of Hugh Capet, according to Twining's *Christian Symbols*, p. 6. Undoubtedly the author is right in attributing most, if not nearly all, the "Hands" to the first Person of the adorable Trinity. One, for instance, shows the table of the law given to Moses. Another, from a Saxon MS., grasps flames, and another spears and arrows.* Yet, while the Hand is shown in benediction on a paten with the Cross, I would still incline to attribute this to Him Who with His Hand blessed the *first* paten, and later lifted up His Hands upon His disciples ere He was parted from them and ascended into heaven.

VIII.
THE LION.

The Lion of the Tribe of Judah was certainly an early emblem of our great Deliverer; but it can hardly be supposed that either the Lion Fonts, so common in

* Ps. xviii. 14.

Suffolk, or the Label Endings of the Porch entrances, almost universal in the same county, are anything but figures of the "British Lion."

On the other hand, a very early Font in S. Mary's, Stafford, has a procession of lions fiercely marching round the base, beneath which are prostrate figures of impish character, while above the lions are strange dragon-like creatures. Here one would think that Baptism was rather figured as the *refuge* from the lion and the dragon, and not as being the way to the *protection* of the Lion of Judah. Of nearly all the later mediaeval lions, Heraldry, and not Hagiology, is probably the parent.

IX

THE PEACOCK.

The Peacock is certainly a religious emblem, and with almost equal assurance we may declare it to belong to our LORD. Martigny says it is an emblem of the Resurrection. S. Augustine says it figures Immortality, because its flesh is incorruptible. Fig. 11, Plate XVIII., is a slightly adapted version of a peacock from the Catacombs. It will be seen that it dominates the Globe, and so shows the victory that overcometh the world.

X.

THE PELICAN.

Surely the most touching of Christian symbols is that of which S. Thomas Aquinas sang—

Pie pelicane, Jesu Domine,
Me immundum munda tuo sanguine.

The legend is fabulous, no doubt the whole idea of the symbol visionary, but it is gospel truth in its teaching. Our LORD, in the Sacrament of His love, feeds us with His own Blood, that our souls may be therein washed. It is Life-Blood and *Living* Blood, and it is given in "His exceeding great love." Moreover, according to the other version of the legend, the Blood of CHRIST is the antidote and cure to the bite of the serpent, and so restores to health, as well as giving food and strength.

Plate XVIII., fig. 5, shows a pelican in its nest, with the blood flowing from the breast towards the young ones below : copied from a Brass in Warbleton Church, dated 1436.

Plate XVI., fig. 5, is from the Tapestry curtain of a fifteenth century Dutch picture, and fig. 6 from the Malvern tiles. In all, the attitude is practically identical, and the three young ones constantly appear, always with open and expectant mouths, waiting for the healing.

XI.

THE PHŒNIX.

This heathen emblem was gladly adopted by the Christians, as the most available symbol ; one, too, likely to appeal to the heathen convert, to whom the

Resurrection was, as we all know, the great stumbling-block. Perhaps no emblem so fully and truly preaches the truth of the Risen Life as this. The destruction of the old body, and the reconstruction of the New, is, so far as I know, only symbolized by this, in all its fulness.

The phœnix of ancient Roman Mythology came from Greece, and almost certainly thither from Persia: the legend and the name alike point eastwards, and one might perhaps regret that now it is practically extinct, and since about the fourteenth century it has never arisen from its ashes.

Fig. 12, Plate XVIII., is a free adaptation of a phœnix in a MS. in the Ashmolean Museum.

XII.

THE PASSION.

"Those dear tokens of His Passion,
Cause of endless exultation
To His ransomed worshippers."

Charles Wesley here expresses the universal sentiment of all Christian artists, of the middle ages, at least. Let Ruskin hold that the contemplation of the Passion is unhealthy. The voice of the ages says clearly that the "Tokens are dear," and that every detail of the way of the Cross, whereby He redeemed the world, may well be figured and blazoned in the Courts of the LORD, every one of them being a part of His Triumph, a trophy of His Victory.

On Plate XXII., fig. 1 is the PILLAR and the cord which bound the SAVIOUR to it.

Fig. 2. The SWORD and the STAFF of one of the band who captured CHRIST in the Garden.

Fig. 3 shows the CROWN OF THORNS with the NAILS. The question of the number of nails (whether three or four) at one time vexed the Church, and gave rise to fierce and bitter controversy. S. Gregory Nazianzen, S. Apollinaris, and others maintained that only three were used. Both these saints above named speak of the Cross as τρυπήλον ξύλον. But S. Cyprian, S. Augustine, Pope Innocent III., and others as vigorously insisted that there were four. The doubt will certainly not be cleared up by existing relics, for there are known to be thirty-two! One of these is incorporated in the iron crown of Charlemagne.

Fig. 4. The SCOURGES.

Fig. 5. The COAT, surmounted by the DICE.

Fig. 6. The REED. This emblem is from stained glass in Malvern Abbey, and is remarkable for the strange and formidable club. It is, so far as I know, a unique example.

Fig. 7. The LANTERN, also from Malvern.

Fig. 10 shows another version of the same from wood-carving.

Fig. 8. The THIRTY PIECES. This, too, is from Malvern glass, and is a beautifully drawn purse.

Fig. 9. The LADDER and the SPONGE.

Fig. 11. The KISS OF JUDAS, again from Malvern. This, too, is almost if not quite unique.

Fig. 12. The FIVE WOUNDS.

Fig. 13. S. Veronica's HANDKERCHIEF from a Cornish bench end.

Fig. 14. The COCK. Another mediaeval cock is also shown, fig. 9, Plate XXIX. from a German Brass; this one is from a *Misericorde* in Peterborough Cathedral.

Fig. 15. The PIERCED HEART, from S. Keverne.*

Fig. 16. The CROSS, with the three nails left in it. Drawn from a Suffolk bench end.

Fig. 17. The HAMMER, as also the nails and PINCERS. Here the pincers are interesting, since they hold one nail in their grip.

On Plate XXIII. are shown several other versions.

Figs 1, 2, 3, 4, 6 are given by Husenbeth as Heraldic *Shields of the Passion*, and are as follows:—

Fig. 1. *Gu.* a Cross, *or*, charged *gouttée de sang*. In the centre ΧΡΣ within a crown of thorns, *ppr.*

Fig. 2. *Arg.* the five wounds in Saltire, in dexter and sinister chief two hands, on base, ditto two feet, and in fesse point the heart, pierced and bleeding, *ppr.* and crowned, *or.*, inscribed respectively well of wisdom, well of mercy, well of grace, well of ghostly comfort, and well of everlasting life.

Fig. 3. *Gu.* a cross within a bordure, *arg.* entwined with a wreath of thorns, *ppr.* In dexter and sinister base, spear, reed, sponge, and three nails, *ppr.* (Mural painting Stow-Bardolph Church.)

Fig. 4. *Arg.* three nails, *sa.* points conjoined within a crown of thorns, *ppr.*

Fig. 5 is from wood-carving in a Cornish bench end, and is not tinted.

Fig. 6. *Arg.* three nails two and one *sa.*

Fig. 10 shows the CUP OF SUFFERING.

Fig. 11 shows the PASSION FLOWER, which emblem is inserted under protest, so to speak.

Of all vulgarised, hackneyed, ill-used decorations, surely this would rank first: and the worst of it is, that while the demand for passion flowers is insatiable, the supply ought to be *impossible;* that is to say, so far as ancient examples are concerned.

It will doubtless astonish some of my readers who have embroidered stoles and book-markers with this wonderful flower, all faithfully copied from a trade catalogue, and guaranteed in the "purest thirteenth century style," to hear that no one this side of the Atlantic had ever dreamed of a passion flower till the Jesuit

---

* The Heart, fig. 12, inscribed "Mercy," is, I think, not the sacred Heart, but that of him who prays for mercy to the LORD.

The Heart with the label enfolding it, Plate XVI., fig. 9, from an ancient font, probably at one time had a "legend" explanatory of its meaning.

Other Emblems of our Lord.

Missionaries in Mexico sent it home. Its reception was but grudging, for the Jesuits were not in universal esteem, and it was generally supposed to be a pious fraud; its symbolism of the twelve apostles, the five wounds, the three nails, and the crown of thorns, being too good to be true!

However, though I earnestly hope never to see another passion flower (and I will *never* draw one again), still in fairness I will give this example of the seventeenth century, drawn in that most beautiful book, *Le Tableau de la Croix*, by F. Mazot, published at Paris in 1651.

Plate XVIII., figs. 1, 2, 3 show the LABEL of our LORD'S "accusation." Fig. 1 is from a painting of Martin Schöngauer, about 1500, and is realistically shown in Hebrew and Greek and Latin. Figs. 2 and 3 are the common abbreviations.

XIII.

THE POMEGRANATE.

On Plate XXIV., fig. 2 shows an example of the sixteenth century. Figs. 4, 5, and 6 are fifteenth century patterns from Tapestry. A rose and pomegranate joined is shown on Plate XXV., fig. 8 (of the Rose); but comparatively few are to be found, save on tapestries and embroidered work. Even here the choice is not so free as at first sight one fancies, for a large proportion of the pomegranates turn out to be pineapples when examined. Moreover, of the later pomegranates, many are royal badges of the Tudors, and not Church emblems at all.

The fruit was, however, an accepted symbol of the richness of Divine Grace, and is either shown split open, with the abundant seeds of new life showing, or it is "voided," and the sacred monogram occupies the space. Certainly, after the rose, it was the favourite flower on which the broiderers showed their skill.

XIV.

THE ROSE.

The rose was certainly not an early emblem in ecclesiastical art, nor can it be regarded as generally used with any very definite or pointed significance. On the other hand, when it once came into vogue it was used with ever-increasing frequency, and its beauty amply atones for its lack of meaning. The rose of Sharon and the lily of the valley are undoubtedly the floral figures of CHRIST that one would expect to see most freely and constantly depicted. But the rose is scarcely ever found before the thirteenth century as a specially religious emblem; and the lily, as is well known to Bible students, was almost certainly a somewhat brilliant scarlet flower, *Lilium Chalcedonicum*, which grows profusely in the Levant, and which (whether white or red) was *never* used as an emblem of the LORD at all.

There can be little doubt that the prevalence of the rose in carving and painting and needlework was mainly the result of its adoption by the adherents of

York and Lancaster as a party badge: red for Lancaster, and white for York. At the fusion of these rival Houses, the rose was first shown red and white, either impaled or quartered or superimposed, and finally without colour (or with no distinctive tint) it became the favourite flower of England, and the most frequent decoration for all manner of work. So the bosses of ceilings were carved, their panels painted, the eyelets of windows were filled, the benches, the tiles, the vestments, and the altar cloths alike were figured and powdered over with roses.

Plates XXIV. and XXV. show several of the innumerable variations of the rose * It will be noticed, I think, that the progress of the conventional rose, like its natural prototype, has followed the same course of development by cultivation, in that it has changed from a single to a double flower; but, though this is the case, its progress has not been quite uniform or regular. Plate XXV., fig. 3, shows, I think, almost the earliest rose, dating as it does from the twelfth century. It is carved on the font of Naseby Church. Fig. 1 is from a tile in Old Cleve Abbey, Somerset, and is somewhat later, probably the end of the thirteenth century. Fig. 2 is from the Brass of Bernard de Lippe, 1340. Fig. 4 (copied from Boutell's Heraldry) shows a rose from the tomb of Prince Edward Tudor. This is, in Heraldic language, *en soleil*, i.e., glorified as by a nimbus with the rays of the sun shining behind it. This was an extremely common representation in Church work of all sorts during the fifteenth and sixteenth centuries. Fig. 5 is from a carved bench end (if my memory serves) in Mullion Church, in Cornwall. It is of immense size, filling the whole width of the end, and measures at least a foot across. Its date is about 1480.

Fig. 6 is from an ancient font in Essex, and its date is about 1400. Fig. 7 is from German wood-carving of the fifteenth century. Fig. 8 is from the late fifteenth century font in Prittlewell Church, Essex, as is also fig. 12. The former shows the rose and pomegranate impaled. Fig. 9 is from the Brass of Albert of Saxony, dated 1500. Fig. 10 appears on three sides of the font in Tolleshunt D'Arcy Church, in Essex. The other sides have plain five-leaved roses very like fig. 6, but without the spike. Fig. 11 is a sixteenth century example of German carving. Fig. 1, Plate XXIV., is of late sixteenth century work, and is copied from stained glass. Fig. 3 is an eccentric example from a monument in Long Ashton Church. Here the spikes of the calix are so elongated that it looks almost more like a star than a rose.

Perhaps the most noteworthy point in these examples is the variation in the number of petals, and the presence or absence of the calix points. It will be seen that the two earliest have both eight leaves: those of the normal or common type have five (or ten when double), but fig. 10 has *seven*, and fig. 7 has *four* for the inner, and eight for the outer rim of petals. We may conclude that here, as in so many other things, there was no hard and fast rule limiting or constraining the

---

* Also some interesting and unusual examples from Tatterhall Church are shown on Plate XIX.

artist; nor any necessary symbolism, figuring the five sacred wounds, or aught else.

The royal rose is beautiful and sweet, in many ways the noblest flower blooming in GOD'S garden, and sanctified by centuries for the beautifying of His House.

BENCH END
PULHAM S MARY

XV.

THE FLEUR DE LYS.

The origin of this emblem appears to be lost in the haze of antiquity, whether we regard it heraldically or symbolically.

Some suppose the common form to have first originated in the spear-head, so far, at least, as it is used as a charge in heraldry.

Whether this be so or not, there is no doubt that a lily *of some sort* has usually been intended. A royal flower, even in the days of Pliny—*(flos rosae nobilitate proximus)*—the lily was regarded as a badge of royalty and dominion, whence its assumption by the Frank princes as their badge.

Clovis, the first Christian king, is credited with its direct reception from heaven by the ministry of an angel; but Louis VII. of France was the first to bear it on his seal, in 1137.

Considered ecclesiastically, it is not certain that the lily, or *fleur de lys*, was the original flower of our Lady, since a tradition makes the pot of flowers, so commonly pictured in the Annunciation, to have been a flowering almond shrub, the rod of Aaron "which bloomed blossoms, and brought forth almonds." *
Certainly, however, from the twelfth century onwards, the lily has been our Lady's flower, and the *fleur de lys* the conventional expression of it.

Whether this be on account of her royal descent, her purity, or in reference to *Virgo puerpera Virgula Jesse* of the Canticles, we cannot be sure; suffice it to say that now-a-days, as in the long past, the lily is the *fleur de lys*.

The form and shape in old representations is of almost infinite variety, though there is a normal type from which such representations never wander past recognition.

The leading idea is a stiff and erect flower, with two petals expanded and curled downwards, while a central one stands erect. Sometimes the points of two other petals show behind the three main members, and sometimes the stamens in place of the latter, or in addition to them. In any case, however, the *triple* form is predominant, and other details are subsidiary. The band which so generally crosses the three petals is not at all easy to understand, since there is nothing in the natural flower to suggest it.

Twelve various forms of the emblem are shown on Plate XXVI.: all authentic, and of various dates.

* Num. xvii. 8.

Figs. 3, 5, and 6 are from tiles of the thirteenth or fourteenth century. Figs. 1, 7, 9 are from stained glass of the fourteenth and fifteenth centuries, and of these I think fig. 7, from Dunmow Church, in Essex, may be taken as, perhaps, the best typical example of the fourteenth century *fleur de lys* attainable. Figs. 2 and 8 are copied from an old number of the *Ecclesiologist*, but the writer gives no clue to their origin, save that they are like many other good things—old.

Fig. 10 (1482) is from a German brass, as is also the sixteenth century example, fig. 12, date 1510. Fig. 11 is from a fifteenth century German wood carving at Munich.

Other emblems of our Lady are :—

*(1) The gilly flower. The shield of arms belonging to New Inn is: *vert* a flower-pot *arg.*, with gilly flowers *gu.*; leaved, *ppr.*, fig. 1, Plate XXVII.

*(2) The flowering lily. The font of Crosthwaite Church has *arg.*, a lily and pot *ppr.* See fig. 2, Plate XXVII. Fig. 11 shows a lily from an old wood-carving.

*(3) The pierced heart; not the fearful object so commonly seen in modern Roman Churches, but the heart pierced with the sword spoken of at the Presentation in the Temple.

The shield, as given by Husenbeth, is blazoned *az.* in fess pt., a heart *ppr.* winged *or.* pierced by a sword *arg.* hilted of the third. See fig. 3.

*(4) The monogram MR. sometimes crowned and sometimes not. Figs. 4 and 6 are two English examples, the first from Blythborough, the second from Malvern Abbey.

*(5) The star. Miriam = "star of the sea," see fig. 8.

(6) The Ark of the Covenant, fig. 7.

*(7) The Mystic Rose, fig. 9.

(8) The Tower of David, fig. 10.

(9) The Gate of Heaven, fig. 12.

(10) The Garden enclosed.

(11) The City of GOD.

(12) The Rod of Jesse.

(13) The lofty cedar.

(14) The Fountain of Living Waters.

(15) The Fountain sealed.

XVI.

THE STAR.

The star which the Magi followed was both the sign of His rising, and the guide to the presence of "the Star that arose out of Jacob."

"I am the Bright and Morning Star," said CHRIST to His servant John in Patmos.

* Of these only those marked with the asterisk can lay any just claim to antiquity; the others are the result of the attempt to apply the Song of Songs, with its varied imagery, to the Virgin Mother of the Beloved Son.

Emblems of Our Lady:

Clearly, the star, in its first signification, indicates our LORD Himself. The star of Bethlehem, as an emblem and a decoration, is ever closely connected with the Nativity. Whether in pictures of the Birth, or the adoration of the new-born King by the kings and shepherds, the star is pretty sure to form part of the composition.

One used to be told that the star *must* have five points, but from the earliest to the latest days the number of rays varied indefinitely. In the cemetery of S. Agnes, for instance, above the heads of the Magi, is a large star of eight points. In the Lateran is one of six; and on an ancient carving in the British Museum the star has thirteen rounded rays. We may safely assert that, as one star differeth from another in the natural heavens, so all that is necessary in depicting a conventional star is to show the lines of light radiating from a centre.

In heraldry, it is true, arbitrary lines are laid down. A *mullet*, Plate XXVIII., fig. 5, has five points, formed by right lines, and no more, unless the number is specifically stated. If it has six or eight the star must be described as a mullet of six points, and so on. Here, however, there is more than a suspicion that the six-pointed mullet is really the rowel of a spur, since the centre is generally pierced.

The *estoile*, fig. 6, on the other hand, has an indefinite number of rays, and they are always *waved*, and not formed by straight lines; frequently the main rays have lesser lines of light between them. See fig. 8. Various stars are shown on this plate, which may be used *ad libitum*. The star is also an emblem of our Lady, Mary, or Miriam, meaning, of course, "star of the sea," but the crown of twelve stars is the commonest attribute of our LORD'S Mother—the woman whose Man-child was caught up to heaven. Nothing but the most abject Protestantism could seek for any escape from the conclusion that she who is pictured in the Apocalypse as crowned with twelve stars, and clothed with the sun and moon, is the Mother of the Bright and Morning Star.

XVII.

THE SUN.

On Plate XXVIII., (figs. 10 and 11), is shown a favourite emblem of the middle ages,* doubtless intended to show our LORD as the *Sol Justitiae*. Very frequently the Sun appears, surrounded by stars, on a vault or ceiling. On either side of the Crucifixion the sun and moon usually appear, more often than not with human faces.

The characteristics of the sun, as distinguished from the star, are the larger centre, and almost universally the alternation of straight and waved rays. This, however, is not always the case, as may be seen by referring to the roses *en soleil*, which are drawn with straight rays.

* Fig. 11 is from a painting by Gheeraert David, 1450.

XVIII.

THE SHIP,

or ark, is generally rather to be interpreted as the Church of CHRIST than as CHRIST Himself. This was regarded (*a*) as the ark of Noah, in which the eight found salvation, and is to be seen in many early representations; or (*b*) it was taken as the ship of S. Peter. Sometimes the ship shows our LORD Himself guiding the barque, with His twelve Apostles rowing it across the seas.

These symbols, however, were displaced by another—the Bride of CHRIST; wherefore the common emblem of the Church is a woman, generally crowned, and holding a sceptre or a cross, and often, too, a chalice.

In the middle ages, however, this figure seldom stood alone, but was nearly always placed in juxtaposition with a blindfolded figure of the synagogue, uncrowned, and with a broken staff, holding the commandments.

Very often these figures were placed on either side of the Crucified LORD, in which case the Church would be receiving the precious Blood from the Pierced Side. For many representations of this emblem see Twining's *Symbols and Emblems*, pp. 128, seq.

XIX.

THE BLESSED SACRAMENT.

Husenbeth gives three varieties of the shield of the Blessed Sacrament. Plate XXIII., fig. 7, is the simplest and most ordinary,—*gu.* a chalice, *or.* Ensigned with the Host, *arg.* Fig. 9, *gu.* Three chalices, *or.* Ensigned with the Host, within a crown of thorns, *ppr.*

A third example shows the three chalices without the thorn-wreath. Of the countless varieties assumed by this emblem it will suffice to refer to a few others figured on Plate XXIX. Fig. 3 is from an early thirteenth century coffin lid. Figs. 4 and 5 are also from thirteenth century grave-stones. It will be noticed that fig. 3 shows the Host at the side of the chalice, and that fig. 5 shows the *paten*. (I know of no other example of this.)

Figs. 6, 7, 19, 27, and 28 are from brasses, English and foreign.

Strangely enough the symbols of the Holy Eucharist are not often found until the middle ages. A few are to be seen in the Catacombs. One, at least, shows a cup with three "crossed" loaves; in another a cup is on a stone altar, with six loaves flanking it. This, in Twining's *Symbols*, is stated to be from a MS. of the eleventh century.

Of the emblem itself, what better could we wish for than the Cup of Blessing and the Bread of Life? Nothing could be desired more simple or more scriptural.

The vine and the wheat are surely neither so eloquent nor so true, for grapes are *not* wine, nor is corn bread.

The vine was, indeed, the plant whence carver and painter alike borrowed

his choicest material to enrich the sanctuary, but he took the vine as the vine of the Church, and showed it, not as cut off for the winepress, but as a luxuriant and fruitful growth, nearly always in a continuous running pattern. Half the old rood-screens in England afford evidence of this. It is true that grapes and wheat are found occasionally in the monuments of the Catacombs, in pictorial representations of the vintage and the harvest, as in the painting of the Good Shepherd in the cemetery of S. Calixtus; but the vine and the corn cutting in this picture are not Christian emblems at all, still less do they figure the daily bread of GOD'S Board.

On Plate XXIV., figs. 10 and 12, I have drawn for such as demand them, ears of wheat and bunches of grapes. The wheat is copied from the tomb of Abbot Wheathamsted, in S. Alban's Abbey. The original has a collar of *hemp* (in place of the scroll), forming the *rebus*—wheat, hemp-sted.

The grapes are copied from the same pattern of tapestry, whence the pelican on Plate XVI. was taken; but though these things are drawn I do not advise their use.

XX.

THE GOOD SHEPHERD.

Here again, while the Catacombs afford scores of examples, after the fifth century there is a blank until this present day, when on Sunday School tickets and Guild cards may be found modernized versions of this ancient figure.

XXI.

THE WHALE.

This is an emblem also forgotten after the first ages of Christianity, until, for a time, it revived in the seventeenth and eighteenth centuries, so vigorously that the Dutch tile-makers divided their favours almost equally between windmills and Jonah's whale.

The sign which He Himself gave, as the *only one*, of His resurrection, might well have been more employed by Christian artists; but the fact remains that it has never found much favour, and is never likely to be again depicted in our Churches.

XXII.

THE WISE MEN'S OFFERINGS.

Three caskets, containing the gold and frankincense and myrrh, or three crowns, are the accepted emblems of the Epiphany.

CHAPTER XIV.

The Holy Angels.

"THE whole company of heaven, and all the powers therein," have been marshalled into various cohorts, commonly known as the "nine orders." From very early times traces of this classification, more or less exact, are found in the Liturgy of the Church.

The common preface of the missal (by no means the least ancient part of it) has *Angeli, Dominationes, Potestates, Virtutes,* et *Seraphim ;* that for Apostles has Angelis et *Archangelis,* cum *Thronis ;* that for the Holy Trinity has, in addition, *Cherubim.* The only order of the accepted nine omitted, is *Principatus.*

The *Te Deum,* less categorically, describes the heavenly host as "all Angels, Cherubim and Seraphim, and Powers."

The accepted classification is of three choirs, each choir being divided into three divisions :—

THE FIRST—CHOIR OF COUNSELLORS.

(*a*) Seraphim.

These are shown with six wings, and generally with eyes both on their wings and bodies. At Chartres a Seraph is shown holding flames of fire in the hands. The distinctive colour of the Seraphim is red ; this indeed is not infrequently the difference between Seraphim and Cherubim, who are oftener than not coloured blue.

(*b*) The Cherubim are generally shown with six wings, though sometimes with four or even two. They carry often an open book or scroll. They may stand on wheels, in reference to the vision of Ezekiel. The Cherub of Sir Joshua Reynolds and that of the old grave-stone are not unrepresented in antiquity. Both paintings and glass afford a large number of such "disembodied spirits," but the more conventional treatment is that given on Plate XXX.

(*c*) Thrones—*Throni.*

The supporters "of the Throne of GOD," are shown carrying thrones or towers.

THE SECOND—CHOIR OF GOVERNORS.

(*a*) Dominations—*Dominationes,* fig. 1.

They are shown clothed, holding either a sword, a sceptre, an orb, or cross. Sometimes they are crowned with a triple crown.

(*b*) Virtues—*Virtutes,* fig. 2.

Are often in full armour. They are said to be possessed of "invincible courage;" they carry battle axes, spears, and other weapons.

(*c*) Powers—*Potestates*.
They sometimes hold devils in chains, and batons in their hands.

THE THIRD—CHOIR OF MESSENGERS.

(*a*) Principalities—*Principatus*,
Hold a lily.

(*b*) Archangels—*Archangeli*,
Of whom there are four, recognised (by name) in the Church;

1. S. Michael, whose name signifies in Hebrew "who is like unto the LORD," often bears a scroll inscribed, *Quis ut Deus*. He tramples on the Devil, piercing him with a cross-tipped spear; he weighs the souls of men in the balance, whence a pair of scales is his emblem.

2. S. Raphael, "GOD is my health," the dear guardian of Tobias, is shown with a pilgrim's staff, a fish, and a wallet.

3. S. Uriel, "GOD is my Light," is he who appeared to Esdras, warning him of presumption if he sought to understand the ways of GOD. His emblems are a scroll and a book.

4. S. Gabriel, the last revealed to mankind, the herald of the Annunciation, "GOD is my strength." "By the message of this angel" we have known the Incarnation of the SON of GOD. He is depicted generally in an alb and cope, or dalmatic, bearing a lily as his emblem, or a shield, with the name of Mary.

If the Archangels are counted as seven, and as identical with the "seven angels before the throne," seen by S. John, and mentioned by S. Raphael to Tobit, three other names are supplied by tradition: (*a*) Chamuel, the angel who wrestled with Jacob, and who appeared to our Blessed LORD, "strengthening Him." He is shown in sacred art bearing a staff and a cup.

(*b*) Jophiel (or *Zophiel*), supposed to have been the angel who drove out our first parents from Eden. He is shown with a flaming sword in his hand.

(*c*) Zadkiel, the angel who stayed the arm of Abraham from slaying his son; he therefore holds a sacrificial knife.

These three additional names do not seem to be quite settled, since another triplet is—*Simiel*, *Oriphiel*, and *Zachariel*.

The Rabbinical teaching is that there are four "Presiding Angels"—Michael, who governs the East; Raphael, the West; Gabriel, the North; and Uriel, the South.

The Koran mentions four "Supporters of the Throne of GOD"—Michael, Gabriel, Raphael, and (instead of Uriel) *Asrafil*, who will blow the trumpet at the Resurrection.

(*c*) Angels—*Angeli*,
Are shown bearing weapons, sceptres, or censers; but also anything under their charge or ministry, or such things as are intended to be brought to our

mind; shields, scrolls, and instruments of music; and above all, the sacred tokens of CHRIST'S Passion are pictured as held by them towards GOD, or towards men.

When looking at any isolated examples, it is useless to try and really differentiate the various orders with exactness, save, perhaps, the *Seraphim* and the *Thrones*.

Nor can any emblem be set down as distinctive of any one order, save the wheel of the *Cherub*, and that is sometimes given to the Seraph also.

A common feature in angelic representation is a tippet or collarette of feathers round the neck. This, I fancy, is to ease the difficulty in joining the clothing and the wings. Often the whole body is feathered, save the head and hands and feet. But again, an angel is shown with nothing superhuman save the wings. A crown, or coronet, or fillet with a jewelled cross frequently circles the head. Sometimes not even wings are drawn to mark the angel as apart from humanity, but there is one thing that can most positively be insisted on. No angel *has sex*. The "lady angels" of latter days are an outrage on faith and reason alike.

The dead mother who grows angel's wings and appears to her sleeping infant, the child that is taken from us and becomes a "cherub," are fantastic and heretical imaginings. Our Divine Redeemer took not on Him the nature of *angels*, but of men; we shall not take on us, or have given to us, the nature of angels either. They that "attain to the resurrection" will not have *wings*, and when it is told us they shall be *as* the angels, the explanation is given at the same time—they *shall not marry*, i.e., all notion of sex is excluded. Wherefore, in all healthy mediaeval angels, nothing is more noticeable than the absence of any distinguishing mark of sex in feature or form. Since Holy Scripture sometimes uses the term "man" as interchangeable with "angel" to show the *stature* and general *figure*, the angel is, perhaps, rather more male than female in likeness, but never markedly so.

On Plate XXX. are shown (*a*) the nine orders of angels, as in the glass of New College, Oxford, which Mr. Parker kindly allowed me to lithograph from his *Kalendar of the Church* in the year 1882, and which I here again reproduce, numbered 3-11.

The two larger angels at the sides are from the Rood Screen of Barton Turf, in Norfolk, figs. 1 and 2. The small sketch of "the preaching angel" is from Mr. Jackson's book.

It may not be superfluous to state that this *exact* classification of angels is not a *mediaeval* encroachment on primitive belief. Dionysius, surnamed the Areopagite (whenever he lived), certainly wrote before the fifth century. Mosheim, the Protestant "historian," politely describes him as "that fanatic who assumed the *name* and *character* of Dionysius the Areopagite. It is not easy to describe how much darkness spread over the minds of many from his writings!"

Yet this "darkness" has been taken as at least a glimmer of the true Light

for 1400 years by the Church, and probably will be when Mosheim is deservedly forgotten.

The nine orders, however, are few of them to be clearly known, unless the names are given. There is absolutely no distinction universally observed. The wings are often more than two; figs. 1 and 2 have each four wings. The Cherubim and Seraphim on the Barton screen have both of them six; while the New College Seraphim and Cherubim have both four. So again the sceptres and censers and spears are quite indifferently distributed among the heavenly host.

The Byzantine manual, as given in Didron's translation, gives the following directions to painters who attempt their portraiture:—

"FIRST ORDER—THRONES, CHERUBIM, SERAPHIM.

"The Thrones are represented as fiery wheels surrounded by wings. These wings are filled with eyes: the whole figure symbolizes a royal Throne.

"The Cherubim are represented with a head only, and two wings.

"The Seraphim with six wings, two of which rise towards the head, two descend to the feet, two are outspread for flight; they bear the flabellum in each hand, with this inscription : ' Holy, holy, holy.' Thus they appeared to the prophet Isaiah.

"How to represent the Tetramorph: They have six wings, angel's face and head, surrounded by nimbus; in their hands they hold the Gospels against their breast. There is an eagle between the two wings that rise above their head, and a lion by the right wing, and an ox by the left. These three symbolic animals look upwards, and hold the Gospels between their feet. Thus the Tetramorphs appeared to the prophet Ezekiel.

"SECOND ORDER, SURNAMED GOVERNORS—DOMINATIONS, VIRTUES, POWERS.

"They wear albs down to the feet, golden girdles, and green stoles. They wear rings of gold upon the right hand, and hold this seal in the left: $\overline{X}$

"THIRD ORDER—PRINCIPALITIES, ARCHANGELS, ANGELS.

"They are represented in soldiers' dress with golden girdles. They hold javelins with hatchets in their hands. The javelins end in lance-heads."

The mediaeval artists of the West being ignorant of these instructions, went their own way; and we must admit their perfect right to do so.

CHAPTER XV.

The Four Evangelists.

It would not be easy to decide whether the earliest types of the Four were the four rivers flowing from the mount of God, or the four books or scrolls.* Probably they were more or less synchronous; but in any case it is clear that they preceded the "evangelistic symbols" as we commonly understand them. About the middle of the fifth century may be taken as the date of their introduction, and concurrently with their symbolic appearance as the living creatures of the Apocalypse, they were portrayed as men, generally accompanied by these symbols. The human representations, I believe, invariably bore the books of their Gospels; and in later times they were shown actually *inscribing* the words of the Gospel with the writer's pen. Plate XXXI., figs. 1 and 2, from a brass, dated 1377.

The figure known as the Tetramorph is an attempt to combine the four in one. The Oriental bias was always rather towards the *Old* Testament view of things, consequently we find this curious six-winged being in the Greek and not the Latin Churches. This has, of course, its theological value, as teaching that there is but one Gospel of Jesus Christ, though the narrative be fourfold. (Plate XXXI., fig. 5.)

Sometimes the actual figures are human, while they bear the *heads* of the living creatures associated with their names. Plate XXXI., fig. 6, and Plate XXXIV., fig. 6.

Here, as in so many other cases, perfect uniformity of interpretation is not to be found. The four, according to the almost universal consent of antiquity, are—

        S. Matthew = an angel (or winged man).
        S. Mark = a lion.
        S. Luke = an ox.
        S. John = an eagle.

Yet, according to S. Augustine, the lion signifies S. Matthew, and the angel S. Mark; his reasons do not appear convincing, while the generally received interpretation commends itself to our minds.

The "face of the man" is S. Matthew's, since he writes the Gospel from its human side. To him the Gospel is the book of the Generation of Jesus Christ, the Son of David. S. Mark gives the voice of the lion in the desert, " Prepare ye the way of the Lord." S. Luke is figured by the sacrificial ox, since he shows us the Christ who takes away our sin; while S. John has the eagle's wings that bear him to the heaven above. See Plate XXXI., fig. 7.

* See Plate XXXIV., fig. 5, from the Catacombs.

Very strange is the *order* in which these symbols appear; strange, that is, considering that the names of the writers are (and have been) uniformly placed—Matthew, Mark, Luke, and John. True, this order is a purely arbitrary one. No one supposes it to be the order of writing, still less an order of *precedence*; but in monumental brasses, windows, carvings, or embroidery, we find the symbols in *every* variety of order conceivable. A few examples will suffice.

On an ancient Altar Cloth at Steeple Aston, the four appear encircling an Agnus Dei.

      S. John. S. Matthew.
      S. Mark. S. Luke.

On a linen Altar Cloth in South Kensington Museum they stand—

      S. John. S. Matthew.
      S. Luke.* S. Mark.

According to Mr. Creeny, Professor Reussens, in his *Elements of Christian Archæology*, states that up to the end of the thirteenth century they stood as (A), and after that as (B), when placed at the four corners of a square brass.

 (A) S. Matthew. | S. John.   (B) S. John. | S. Matthew.
    S. Mark. | S. Luke.   S. Mark. | S. Luke.

This does not settle the question, however, since on crosses they stand diamond wise, and then again the order is very uncertain.

The symbols, too, have been sometimes appropriated for the four Archangels or the four Major Prophets; also to four Doctors of the Western Church—S. Jerome, S. Augustine, S. Ambrose, and S. Gregory. The two former interpretations are those of the Jewish doctors, whose horizon was limited by the vision of the kingdom of Messias; while the application of these four signs to the Doctors of the Church is not so easily to be understood, seeing that it means taking them from the Holy Evangelists to bestow them elsewhere.

The aptness of the symbolism is the more strongly felt when we consider how by CHRIST "both in the Old and New Testament life is offered to mankind" (Art. VII., Prayer Book).

Therefore in the vision of Ezekiel, the four living creatures with four faces, have been fitly identified with the four creatures round the throne, as seen by S. John. Though if Ezek. i. 5 be compared with Apoc. iv. 7, we are confronted with the difference of the appearance. While Ezekiel saw "each with four faces," S. John saw each with *one*.

So while the Tetramorph was sometimes figured, the usual method is to show but one face to each creature.

Where the scrolls are held by them they are sometimes blank, sometimes they bear the Evangelists' names—

  Scus matthaeus : scus marcus : scus lucas : S. Johannes.

      * Plate XXXI., fig. 4.

And perhaps as often, the initial words of their respective Gospels;

1. *Liber generationis Jesu Xti.* or *Liber generationis.*
2. *Initium Evangelii Jesu Xti.* or *Initium Evangelii.*
3. *Fuit in diebus Herodis* or *Fuit in diebus.*
4. *In principio erat verbum* or *In principio.*

The four large examples on Plate XXXIV., figs. 1, 2, 3, 4, are from a brass dated 1487 in Ypres: the small symbol of S. Mark from a brass dated 1452.

CHAPTER XVI.

The Holy Apostles.

THE twelve foundations of the city, as enumerated in the Gospels, cannot be the same twelve as seen by S. John the Divine in his vision, since one by transgression had fallen, and the foundations had to be re-laid.

It is clear, therefore, that the twelve of the Apocalypse consist of the faithful eleven and S. Matthias.

S. Paul, however, though he disclaims building on another foundation, or taking to himself the honour of the twelve first stones, still distinctly claims to be an Apostle. "Am I not one?" he asks; and, "Do I come short of the chiefest of them?"

The position of the great preacher of the Gentiles has a little complicated the question of "*who* are the twelve?" when we see twelve figures representing the Apostles.

When, as so often is the case, they bear scrolls with "articles of the belief" inscribed, it is fairly clear that the figures are:

(1) S. Peter—*Credo in Deum Patrem omnipotentem, Creatorem coeli et terrae,*

(2) S. Andrew—*et in Jesum Christum Filium ejus unicum, Dominum nostrum.*

(3) S. James Major—*Qui conceptus est de Spiritu Sancto, natus ex Maria Virgine.*

(4) S. John—*Passus sub Pontio Pilato, crucifixus, mortuus, et sepultus.*

(5) S. Philip—*Desendit ad inferos; tertia die resurrexit a mortuis.*

(6) S. James Minor—*Ascendit ad coelos, sedet ad dextram Dei Patris omnipotentis.*

(7) S. Thomas—*Inde venturus est judicare vivos et mortuos.*

(8) S. Bartholomew—*Credo in Spiritum Sanctum,*

(9) S. Matthew—*Sanctam Ecclesiam Catholicam, sanctorum communionem,*

(10) S. Simon—*Remissionem peccatorum,*

(11) S. Jude—*Carnis resurrectionem,*

(12) S. Matthias—*et vitam aeternam.*

This order, at least, is that fixed by the Roman Canon, and it is not worth while attempting to discuss the identity of S. Bartholomew with Nathaniel, nor of Thaddaeus and Lebbaeus with Jude. But when, as so often is the case, S. Paul is *distinctly* added to the sacred college, the question naturally arises, who should be displaced? S. Matthias, S. Jude, or S. James Minor sometimes are omitted, and S. John Baptist inserted; occasionally, too, S. Luke or S. Mark. Lest this should seem a very free handling of the sacred record, we must remember that, even in Scripture the stress is laid on the *number*, and not the *names* of the twelve.

So much is this the case, that in one passage S. Paul says our LORD " was seen . . . of the *twelve*," * when, as a matter of fact, there were only eleven, since Matthias was not elected.

This may be seen from the earliest representations of the Apostles as twelve sheep, absolutely without individual character; or as twelve human figures with twelve sheep, also unmarked, except in the case of one or two bearing scrolls.

In the Church of S. Agatha, Rome, is a mosaic containing the twelve Apostles, named; S. Petrus, S. Andreas, S. Joannes, S. Thomas, S. Matteus, S. Bartolomeus, S. Jacobus Alpei, S. Simon Zelotes, S. Jacobus, S. Judas Jacobi, S. Philippus, S. Paulus.

In this example S. Matthias is replaced by S. Paul. The date of the mosaic is the middle of the fifth century. None of the figures have, however, any mark except S. Peter, who bears a key. Another example (1299) shows eleven doves surrounding the CHRIST, on the great crucifix in the apse of S. Clement's, Rome.

The twelve figures on Plate XXXII. and XXXIII. are from pictures of the twelve by Martin Schoengauer. Here, again, S. Paul has taken the place of S. Matthias, but the remainder are not easily to be identified.

The twelve quaint figures on Plate XXXIV. are from an old woodcut of the fifteenth century. Here, at least, there is no obscurity, since each Apostle has his emblem clearly defined, and the names are added to make assurance doubly sure: S. Peter, S. Andrew, S. James the More, S. Johan, S. Thomas, S. James ye Less, S. Phylippe, S. Barthymew, S. Mathewe, S. Jude, S. Symon, S. Mathyas.

Perhaps the commonest position for pictures of the twelve (in England) was the lower wall of the rood screen; or in niches on the exterior of the west end, there were statues, as at Wells Cathedral; or in the windows of the nave. In Germany the twelve are often found in panels behind the stalls of the choir, the twelve prophets facing them on the cantoris side, and the doctors of the Church over the Returned stalls at the choir entrance.

There is, however, no appropriation of seats or places; and the figures of the Apostles are found anywhere and everywhere.

Often they appear in wood-carving as busts. See Plate XXXI., fig. 8, from an old German wood-carving.

Their emblems will be found in the List of Emblems, pp. 154–160, arranged alphabetically among the other saints.

The *illustrated* emblems, and the shields of arms pertaining to some of them, will be found described in Chap. XXIII., separate from the rest of the saints, whose emblems and shields follow after.

* 1 Cor. xv. 5.

CHAPTER XVII.
The Twelve Prophets.

THE forerunners of the Apostles have been commonly accepted as identical with the "prophets and apostles" mentioned in Ephesians ii. 20; but as S. Paul places the apostles first in mentioning the foundation of the apostles and prophets, he probably meant the prophets of the new dispensation, of whom he mentions several in the Acts (xiii. 1) —"Certain prophets and teachers, as Barnabas and Simeon Niger, and Lucius, and Manaen." Nevertheless, in post-apostolic days "the prophets" were the old twelve, who spake of CHRIST and His sufferings, and of the Law of GOD.*

Of these, the four greater—Isaiah, Jeremiah, Ezekiel, and Daniel—are the more commonly portrayed, but the other eight are often found.

Emblems of certain of them are shown, but the commoner plan is to give each prophet a scroll of his own witness to the truth :—

Amos—a shepherd's crook.
Daniel—a lion; a ram with four horns.
Ezekiel—a turreted gateway in his hand; a plan of the new Jerusalem.
Isaiah—a saw; clothed in a sack; holding S. Matthew on his shoulder.
Jeremiah—a wand in the hand.
Joel—lions around him.
Obadiah—a pitcher of water and loaves.
Malachi—an angel.
Zechariah—a temple building; a stone covered with eyes.

Other of the patriarchs are often known by various emblems; e.g.

Adam—a spade.
Abraham—a knife and brazier of fire.
David—a harp; a sling and stones; the head of Goliath.
Elias—scroll and red robes; fiery chariot; a sword.
Elisha—a two-headed eagle on his shoulder.
Gideon—a fleece of wool.
Jonah—a whale; a ship; a gourd growing.
Joseph—a purse.
Melchizedek—as priest and king.
Moses—the tables of the Law; a rod; horns of light; the burning bush; a rock.
Noah—the ark; a dove with olive branch; an oar.
Sampson—the gates of the city; the jaw-bone of an ass.
Seth—three seeds of the tree of life; thread bound thrice round his thumb.
Zacharias—a lighted taper.

* The goodly fellowship of the prophets in the *Te Deum* are clearly those of the old dispensation.

CHAPTER XVIII.

The Calendar.

In the list of emblems, pp. 154-160, the calendar of the present Book of Common Prayer is taken as the *basis*, but copious additions are made from other sources. This was necessary, if the names of many common English dedications were to be included.

The calendar of the First Prayer Book of Edward VI. contained only twenty-five days, which are virtually our present red letter days, with the addition of S. Mary Magdalene (for which a Service was provided).

The Second Book had twenty-seven. S. Laurence, S. George, and S. Clement were added, but S. Mary Magdalene was taken out. No *Services*, however, were given for the three days above mentioned.

The various books of Elizabeth's reign, consisting of Prayer Books and Primers, etc., had calendars of surprising variety. Some most startling insertions appeared "under Royal authority" (be that worth what it may). The re-introduction of All Souls and the Assumption is noteworthy, but S. Thomas à Becket is an astounding disrespect to Elizabeth's sainted father, and the *Chair of S. Peter*, February 22nd,* is simply incomprehensible.

The fullest and most complete of these calendars is that in the *Preces Privatae*, 1564. Its origin is not very clear, since it neither corresponds with the Roman, the Sarum, nor the other old English lists. It has a few coincidences with both, and also here and there with the old French one, but speaking generally it is decidedly eclectic.

Perhaps the most generally useful course will be to give the Roman and Old English Calendars side by side, and the reader will thereby see how many names were "written in the Book of Life" by the hands of our forefathers ; and also how widely different were the Commemorations of old England from those of Rome. It is possible that in one or other of these two calendars, there may be the patron saint of some parish otherwise unknown, and the traditional date of the parish feast will in all likelihood be found to correspond with the date here given.

This, however, is not universally true, since nothing is commoner than to find a variation of a day or more between one "edition" of a calendar and another.

The shifting of S. Alban's day from June 22nd to June 17th in our own Prayer Book, is by no means a solitary example of this seemingly capricious transference of feasts.

* This date is given in the Roman Calendar as S. Peter's Chair at *Antioch*, while January 18th is S. Peter's Chair at *Rome*.

The Calendar.

ROMAN CALENDAR.

JANUARY.

1. Circumcision of our LORD
2. Octave of S. Stephen
3. Octave of S. John
4. Octave of Holy Innocents
5. Vigil of Epiphany, S. Telesphorus, P.M.
6. Epiphany of our LORD
7. Of the Octave
8. Of the Octave
9. Of the Octave
10. Of the Octave
11. Of the Octave. S. Hyginus, P.M.
12. Of the Octave
13. Octave of the Epiphany
14. S. Hilary, B.C. S. Felix, M.
15. S. Paul, H. S. Maurus, Ab.
16. S. Marcellus, P.M.
17. S. Anthony, Ab.
18. S. Peter's Chair at Rome. S. Prisca, V.M.
19. SS. Marius, &c., MM.
20. SS. Fabian and Sebastian, MM.
21. S. Agnes, V.M.
22. SS. Vincent and Anastasius, MM.
23. Desponsation of B. V. Mary
24. S. Timothy, B.M.
25. Conversion of S. Paul
26. S. Polycarp, B.M.
27. S. John Chrysostom, B.C.
28. S. Raymund of Pennafort, C.
29. Francis of Sales, B.C.
30. S. Martina, V.M.
31. S. Peter Nolasco, C.

FEBRUARY.

1. S. Ignatius, B.M.
2. Purification of B. V. Mary
3. S. Blaize, B.C.
4. S. Andrew Corsini, B.C.
5. S. Agatha, V.M.
6. S. Dorothy, V.M.
7. S. Romuald, Abbot
8. S. John of Matha, C.
9. S. Apollonia, V.M.
10. S. Scholastica, V.
11.
12.
13.
14. S. Valentine, M.
15. SS. Faustinus and Jovita, MM.
16.
17.
18. S. Simeon, B.M.
19.
20.
21.
22. S. Peter's Chair at Antioch
23. S. Peter Damian, B.C.D.
24. S. Matthias, Ap.
25.

OLD ENGLISH CALENDAR.

JANUARY.

S. Elvan, B.C.
Thousand Martyrs.
S. Fintan, Ab.
S. Melorus, M.
S. Edward, K.C.
S. Peter, A.B.
S. Cedda, B.C.
S. Wulfine, B.C.
S. Brithwald, B.C.
S. Adrian, Ab.
S. Egwin, B.C.
S. Bennet Biscop, Ab.
S. Kentigern, B.C.
SS. Maura and Bridget, VV.MM.
S. Ita, V.
S Henry, Hermit, C.
S. Caradoc, Hermit, C.
S. Deicola, Hermit, C.
S. Wulstan, B.C.
S. Richard, Hermit, C.
S. Malcallan, Ab.
S. Maimbodus, M.
S. Theorithgith, V.
S. Cadoc, Ab.
S. Paul, Hermit.
S. Bathildis, Qu.
S. Algina, V.
S. Sexulph, B.C.
S. Gildas the Elder, C.
S. Gildas the Younger, C.
S. Wilgis, Ab.

FEBRUARY.

S. Bridget, V.
S. Laurence, B.C.
S. Wereburge, V.
S. Gilbert, C.
S. Indractus, &c., MM.
S. Inas, K.C.
S. Augulus, B.M.
S. Elfleda, V.
S. Thelian, B.C.
S. Trumwin, B.C.
S. Cedmon, C.
S. Edilwald, C.
S. Ermenilda, Qu.
S. Fechinus, Ab.
S. Sigfrid, B.C.
S. Oswy, K.C.
S. Finan, B.C.
S. Ethelstan, B.C.
S. Acca, B.C.
S. Ulric, C.
S. Cenibert, B.C.
SS. Ethnen and Fidelmia, VV.
S. Milburge, V.
S. Ethelbert, K.C.
S. Furseus, Ab.

ROMAN CALENDAR.
FEBRUARY—(continued).

26	
27	
28	
29	

MARCH.

1	
2	
3	
4	S. Casimir, C.
5	
6	
7	S. Thomas of Aquin, C.D.
8	S. John of God, C.
9	S. Frances, Wid.
10	Forty Martyrs
11	
12	S. Gregory the Great, P.C.D.
13	
14	
15	
16	
17	S. Patrick, B.C.
18	S. Gabriel, Archangel
19	S. Joseph, C.
20	
21	S. Benedict, Ab.
22	
23	
24	
25	Annunciation of B.V. Mary
26	
27	
28	
29	
30	
31	

APRIL.

1	
2	S. Francis of Paula, C.
3	
4	S. Isidore, B.C.
5	S. Vincent Ferrer, C.
6	
7	
8	
9	
10	
11	S. Leo the Great, P.C.D.
12	
13	S. Hermenegild, M.
14	SS. Tiburtius, Valerianus, and Maximus,
15	[MM.
16	
17	S. Anicetus, P.M.
18	
19	

OLD ENGLISH CALENDAR.
FEBRUARY—(continued).

S. Milwida, V.
S. Elvius, B.C.
S. Oswald, B.C.

MARCH.

S. David, B.C.
S. Chad, B.C.
S. Winwaloe, Ab.
S. Owen, C.
S. Piran, B.C.
S. Fridolin, Ab.
S. Esterwin, Ab.
S. Felix, Ap. of the East Angles.
S. Alured, Ab.
S. Himelin, Hermit.
S. Lietphard, B.M.
S. Brian, K.M.
S. Cungarus, Hermit.
S. Ceoluph, K.C.
S. Aristobulus, B.M.
S. Adaman, C.
S. Patrick, B.C.
S. Edward, K.M.
S. Alemund, M.
S. Cuthbert, B.C.
S. Herebert, H.C.
S. Hamund, B.M.
SS. Finguar and Piala, and 777 Martyrs.
S. Lanfranc, B.C.
S. William of Norwich, M.
S. Alfwould, B.C.
S. Rupert, B.C.
S. Albert, B.C.
S. Gelasius, B.C.
S. Patton, B.C.
SS. Adrian and Cadoc, CC.

APRIL.

S. Agilbert, B.C.
S. Ebba, etc., MM.
S. Richard, B.C.
S. Gundleius, K.H.
S. Asser, B.C.
S. Elstan, B.C.
S. Bernac, Ab.
S. Lethard, B.C.
SS. Gisla and Richtrude, VV.
S. Paternus, C.
S. Guthlac, Hermit.
S. Mechtildes, Wid.
S. Elfleda, Wid.
S. Ethelwolf, K.C.
S. Paternus, B.C.
S. Maxentia, V.M.
S. Stephen, Ab.
S. Erard, B.C.
S. Alphege, Ab. M.

The Calendar.

ROMAN CALENDAR.
APRIL—(continued).

20
21 S. Anselm, B.C.
22 SS. Soter and Caius, PP.MM.
23 S. George, M.
24 S. Fidelis, M.
25 S. Mark, Ev.
26 SS. Cletus and Marcellinus, PP.MM.
27
28 S. Vitalis, M.
29 S. Peter, M.
30 S. Catharine of Sienna, V.

MAY.

1 SS. Philip and James, App.
2 S. Athanasius, B.C.D.
3 Finding of the Holy Cross
4 S. Monica, Wid.
5 S. Pius V., P.C.
6 S. John bef. the Latin Gate
7 S. Stanislas, B.M.
8 Apparition of S. Michael
9 S. Gregory Nazianzen, B.C.D.
10 S. Antoninus, B.C.
11
12 SS. Nereus, Achilleus, Domitilla, and
13   [Pancras
14 S. Boniface, M.
15
16 S. John Nepomucen, M.
17 S. Ubaldus, B.C.
18 S. Venantius, M.
19 S. Peter Celestin, P.C.
20 S. Bernardin, C.
21
22
23
24 Our B. Lady, Help of Christians
25 S. Mary Magdalen of Pazzis, V.
26 S. Philip Neri, C.
27 S. John, P.M.
28 S. Gregory VII., P.C.
29
30 S. Felix, P.M.
31 S. Petronilla, V.

JUNE.

1
2 SS. Marcellinus, Peter, and Erasmus, MM.
3
4
5
6 S. Norbert, B.C.
7
8
9 SS. Primus and Felicianus, MM.
10 S. Margaret, Qu.
11 S. Barnabas, Ap.
12 S. John a Facundo, C.

OLD ENGLISH CALENDAR.
APRIL—(continued).

S. Cedwal, K.C.
S. Anselm, B.C.
S. Bristan, B.C.
S. Etheldred, K.C.
S. Mellitus, B.C.
S. Egbert, Ab. C.
S. Leofric, B.C.
S. Walburge, Abbess.
S. Ivo, B.C.
S. Paul, B.C.
S. Erconwald, B.C.

MAY.

S. Asaph, B.C.
S. Ultan, Ab.
S. Walter, Ab.
S. Etheldred, K.C.
S. Richard, K.C.
S. Edbert, B.C.
S. John of Beverley, B.C.
S. Wire, C.
S. Beatus, C.
S. Henry, B.C.
S. Fremund, M.
S. Remigius, B.C.
S. Merwina, Abbess.
S. Editha, V.
S. Dympna, V.M.
S. Simon Stock, C.
S. Carantoc, C.
S. Sewal, B.C.
S. Dunstan, B.C.
S. Ethelbert, K.M.
S. Godric, Hermit.
S. Constantine the Great, Emp.
S. William, M.
S. Robert, B.C.
S. Aldelm, B.C.
S. Augustin, Ap. of England, C.
S. Bede, C.
S. Theocus, Hermit.
S. Ergontha, V.
S. Hienna, V.
S. Guithelinus, B.C.

JUNE.

S. Wistan, M.
S. Malcolm, K.C.
S. Pega, V.
S. Petroc, Ab.
S. Boniface, B.M.
S. Gudwall, B.C.
S. Robert, Ab.
S. William, B.C.
S. Columba, Ab.
S. Margaret, Qu.
S. Egbert, K.C.
S. Cunera, V.M.

ROMAN CALENDAR.

JUNE - (continued).

13 S. Anthony of Padua, C.
14 S. Basil the Great, B.C.D.
15 SS. Vitus, Modestus, and Crescentia, MM.
16 .
17 .
18 SS. Marcus and Marcellianus, MM.
19 S. Juliana Falconieri, V.
20 S. Silverius, P.M.
21 S. Aloysius, C.
22 S. Paulinus, B.C.
23 .
24 Nativity of S. John Baptist
25 Of the Octave of Nat. of S. John
26 SS. John and Paul, MM.
27 Of the Octave
28 S. Leo, P.C.
29 SS. Peter and Paul, App.
30 Commemoration of S. Paul

JULY.

1 Octave of S. John Baptist
2 Visitation of B. V. Mary
3 Of the Octave of SS. Peter and Paul
4 Of the Octave
5 Of the Octave
6 Octave of SS. Peter and Paul
7 .
8 S. Elizabeth, Qu.
9 .
10 Seven Brothers and SS. Rufina and Secunda,
11 S. Pius, P.M. [MM.
12 S. John Gualbert, Ab.
13 S. Anacletus, P.M.
14 S. Bonaventure, B.C.D.
15 S. Henry, Emp. C.
16 Our Blessed Lady of Mt. Carmel
17 S. Alexius, C.
18 S. Camillus de Lellis, C.
19 Vincent of Paul, C.
20 S. Jerom Emilian, C.
21 S. Praxedes, V.
22 S. Mary Magdalen, Pent.
23 Apollinaris, B.M.
24 S. Christina, V.M.
25 S. James the Great, Ap.
26 Ann, Mother of B.V.M.
27 S. Pantaleon, M.
28 SS. Nazarius, Celsus, &c., MM.
29 S. Martha, V.
30 SS. Abdon and Sennen, MM.
31 S. Ignatius, C.

AUGUST.

1 S. Peter's Chains
2 S. Alphonsus Liguori, B.C.
3 Finding of S. Stephen, M.
4 S. Dominic, C.
5 Our Blessed Lady ad Nives

OLD ENGLISH CALENDAR.

JUNE—(continued).

S. Odulphus, C.
S. Brandan, Ab. C.
S. Eadburga, V.
S. Mayne, Ab.
S. Botolph, Ab.
S. Adolph, B.C.
S. Burjene, V.
Translation of SS. Edward and Oswald,
S. Egelmond, M. [KK.MM.
S. Alban, Protomartyr of Britain.
S. Ediltrude, Qu. V.
S. Bartholomew, C.
S. Amphibalus, C.
S. Adelbert, C.
S. Sezinus, B.C.
S. Sethrida, V.
S. Hugh, M.
S. Theodatus, B.C.

JULY.

SS. Julius and Aaron, MM.
S. Oudock, B.C.
S. Guthagon, Hermit.
S. Odo, B.C.
S. Modwena, V.
S. Sexburge, Qu. Ab.
Translation of S. Thomas of Cant.
S. Edgar, K.C.
S. Ethelburga, Qu. Ab.
S. Grimbald, Ab.
S. Withburge, V.
S. Kilian, &c., MM.
S. Mildreda, V.
S. Marcellinus, C.
S. Swithun, B.C.
S. Osmund, B.C.
S. Kenelm, K.M.
S. Edburge, V.
S. Dimancus, C.
S. Alfwitha, Qu.
S. Ethelburga, V.
S. Kenulph, K.C.
S. Vodinus, B.C.
SS. Rufinus and Ulfadus, MM.
S. Adlar, B.M.
S. Christina, V.
S. Joseph of Arimathea, C.
S. Sampson, B.C.
SS. Germanus and Lupus, BB.CC.
S. Tatwinus, B.C.
S. Neot, C.

AUGUST.

S. Ethelwold, B.C.
S. Kined, Hermit.
S. Domitius, C.
S. Ivo, B.C.
S Oswald K.M.

The Calendar.

ROMAN CALENDAR.
AUGUST—(continued).

6 Transfiguration of our LORD
7 S. Cajetan, C.
8 SS. Cyriacus, &c., MM.
9 S. Romanus, M.
10 S. Laurence, M.
11 SS. Tiburtius and Susanna, MM.
12 S. Clare, V.
13 SS. Hippolytus and Cassian, MM.
14 S. Eusebius, C.
15 Assumption of B. V. Mary
16 S. Hyacinth, C.
17 Octave of S. Laurence, M.
18 S. Agapitus, M.
19 Of the Octave of Assumption
20 S. Bernard, Ab. D.
21 S. Jane Frances, W.
22 Octave of the Assumption
23 S. Philip Benitius, C.
24 S. Bartholomew, Ap.
25 S. Louis, K.C.
26 S. Zephyrinus, P.M.
27 S. Joseph Calasanctius, C.
28 S. Augustin, B.C.D.
29 Beheading of S. John Baptist
30 S. Rose of Lima, V.
31 S. Raymund Nonnatus, C.

SEPTEMBER.

1 S. Giles, Ab. C.
2 S. Stephen, K.C.
3
4
5 S. Laurence Justinian, B.C.
6
7
8 Nativity of B. V. Mary
9 S. Gorgonius, M.
10 S. Nicholas of Tolentinum, C.
11 SS. Protus and Hyacinth, MM.
12 Of the Octave of the Nativity
13 Of the Octave
14 Exaltation of the Holy Cross
15 Octave of the Nativity
16 SS. Cornelius and Cyprian, MM.
17 Impression of Stigmas of S. Francis
18 S. Joseph of Curpertino, C.
19 SS. Januarius, &c., MM.
20 SS. Eustachius, &c., MM.
21 S. Matthew, Ap. Ev.
22 S. Thomas of Villanova, B.C.
23 S. Linus, P.M.
24 Our Blessed Lady of Mercy
25
26 SS. Cyprian and Justina, MM.
27 SS. Cosmas and Damian, MM.
28 S. Wenceslas, M.
29 Dedication of S. Michael
30 S. Jerome, C.D.

OLD ENGLISH CALENDAR.
AUGUST—(continued).

S. Henry, B.C.
S. Claudia Rufina.
S. Brice, B.C.
S. Hugh, B.C.
S. Henry, VI., K.C.
S. Gilbert, B.C.
S. Alcuin, Ab.
S. Wigbert, M.
S. Werenfrid, C.
S. Margaret, V.
S. Alexander, C.
S. Thomas, C.
S. Helen, Empress.
S. Clitaneus, K.M.
S. Oswin, K.M.
SS. Arwald Brothers, MM.
S. Arnulph, Hermit.
S. Justinian, M.
S. Alice, V.
S. Ebba, Abbess.
S. Bregwin, B.C.
S. Decuman, Hermit.
S. Harmacharus, B.C.
S. Sebbe, K.C.
S. Fiaker, C.
S. Aidan, B.C.

SEPTEMBER.

S. Alphege, B.C.
S. Adamen, Ab.
S. Mansuetus, B.C.
S. Swibert, B.C.
S. Altho, Ab.
S. Magnus, Ab.
S. Leofgar, B.C.
S. Ethelburga, Qu., Abbess.
S. Osmanna, V.
S. Orgerus, C.
S. Wulfhildis, V.
S. Eanswide, V.
S. Turgotus, B.C.
S. Gelduinus, C.
S. Editha, V.
S. Ninian, B.C.
SS. Stephen and Socrates, MM.
S. Wenoch, C.
S. Theodore, B.C.
S. Heriswide, Qu.
S. Gurval, B.C.
S. Hia, V
S. Alfwold, K.M.
S. Winnibald, C.
S. Theodoric, &c., MM.
S. Hedda, and eighty-four Monks, MM.
S. Sigebert, K.M.
S. Lioba, V.
S. Roger, B.C.
S. Honorius, B.C.

ROMAN CALENDAR.	OLD ENGLISH CALENDAR.
OCTOBER.	OCTOBER.
1 S. Remigius, B.C.	S. Wasnulph, C.
2 The Holy Angels Guardians	S. Thomas of Hereford, B.C.
3	SS. Ewald, Brothers, MM.
4 S. Francis of Assissium, C.	S. Edwin, K.M.
5 SS. Placidus, etc., MM.	S. Wilfrid the Younger, B.C.
6 S. Bruno, C.	S. Ivy, C.
7 S. Mark, P.C.	S. Osyth, Qu. M.
8 S. Bridget, W.	S. Keyna, V.
9 SS. Dionysius, Rusticus, and Eleutherius,	S. Robert Gros-tête, B.C.
10 S. Francis Borgia, C. [MM.	S. Paulinus, B.C.
11	S. Ethelburga, V.
12	S. Wilfrid the Elder, B.C.
13 S. Edward, K.C.	Translation of S. Edward, K.C.
14 S. Callistus, P.M.	S. Burchard, B.C.
15 S. Teresa, V.	S. Tecla, V.
16	S. Lullus, B C.
17 S. Hedwiges, W.	SS Ethelbright and Ethelred, Brothers, MM.
18 S. Luke, Ev.	S. Ethbin, C.
19 S. Peter of Alcantara, C.	S. Frideswyde, V.
20 S. John Cantius, C.	SS. Kenred and Offa, KK.CC.
21 S. Hilarion, Ab.	S. Ursula and Companions, VV. MM.
22	S. Melanius, B.C.
23	S. Edilburge, V.
24 S. Raphael, Archangel	S. Maglorius, B.C.
25 SS. Chrysanthus and Daria, MM.	SS. Valeria and Pollena, VV.
26 S. Evaristus, P.M.	SS. Eata, B., and Hagulstad, C.
27 Vigil	S. Rumwald, B.C.
28 SS. Simon and Jude, App.	S. Alfred, K.C.
29	S. Elfleda, V.
30	S. Egelnoth, B.C.
31 Vigil	S. Foillain, B. M.
NOVEMBER.	NOVEMBER.
1 All Saints.	S. Cissa, V.
2 All Souls.	S. Vulganius, B.C.
3 Of the Octave of All Saints	S. Winefred, V.M.
4 S. Charles, B.C.	S. Clarus, M.
5 Of the Octave	S. Malachy, B.C.
6 Of the Octave	S. Iltutus, C.
7 Of the Octave	S. Willebrord, B.C.
8 Octave of All Saints	S. Willehad, B.C.
9 Dedication of Church of our SAVIOUR	S. Kebius, B.C.
10 S. Andrew Avellini, C.	S. Justus, B.C.
11 S. Martin, B.C.	S. Jeron, M.
12 S. Martin, P.M.	S. Lebvin, C.
13 S. Didacus, C.	S. Dubritius, B.C.
14	S. Laurence, B.C.
15 S. Gertrude, V.	S. Malo, B.C.
16	S. Edmund, B.C.
17 S. Gregory Thaumaturgus, B.C.	S. Hugh, B.C.
18 Dedication of Church of SS. Peter and	S. Fulco, C.
19 S. Elizabeth, W. [Paul	S. Ermenburga, Qu. Abbess.
20 S. Felix of Valois, C.	S. Edmund, K.M.
21 Presentation of B. V. Mary	S. Columban, Ab.
22 S. Cecily, V.M.	S. Bega, V.
23 S. Clement, P.M.	S. Eadsinus, B.C.
24 S. John of the Cross, C.	S. Christina, V.
25 S. Catharine, V.M.	S. Alnoth, M.

ROMAN CALENDAR.	OLD ENGLISH CALENDAR.
NOVEMBER—*(continued)*.	NOVEMBER—*(continued)*.
26 S. Peter, B.M.	S. Egbert, C.
27	S. Oda, V.
28	S. Edwold, C.
29 S. Saturninus, M.	S. Baruc, C.
30 S. Andrew, Ap.	S. Theanus, B.C.
DECEMBER.	DECEMBER.
1	S. Virgilius, B.C.
2 S. Bibiana, V.M.	S. Weedc, Ab.
3 S. Francis Xavier, C.	S. Lucius, K.C.
4 S. Peter Chrysologus, B.C.	S. Birinus, B.C.
5 S. Sabbas, Ab.	S. Eanfled, Qu.
6 S. Nicholas, B.C.	S. Congellus, Ab.
7 S. Ambrose, B.C.D.	S. Oswald, B.C.
8 Conception of B.V. Mary	S. Agatha, Qu.
9 Of the Octave of the Conception	S. Elgiva, Qu.
10 S. Melchiades, P.M.	S. Daniel, B.C.
11 S. Damasus, P.C.	S. Boysil, Ab.
12 Of the Octave	S. Elfreda, V.
13 S. Lucy, V.M.	S. Judocus, Hermit.
14 Of the Octave	S. Edburge, V.
15 Octave of Conception of B.V.M.	S. Hilda, V.
16 S. Eusebius, B.M.	S. Colman, M.
17	S. Titta, V.
18	S. Daniel, B.C.
19	S. Macarius, Ab.
20 Vigil	S. Mathilda, Qu.
21 S. Thomas, Ap.	S. Eustachius, C.
22	S. Hildelida, V.
23	S. Ithwara, V.M.
24 Vigil	S. Ruthius, C.
25 Nativity of our LORD	S. Gregory, C.
26 S. Stephen, M.	S. Tatheus, C.
27 S. John, Ap. Ev.	S. Gerard, C.
28 Holy Innocents	S. Walstan, C.
29 S. Thomas of Canterbury, B.M.	S. Thomas of Canterbury, B.M.
30 Of the Sunday within Octave of Nativity	S. Ralph, Ab.
31 S. Sylvester, P.C.	S. Ethernan, C.

☦

For a fuller comparative view of calendars, the reader is referred to the various editions of the post Reformation *Services* and *Primers* published by the Parker Society; the appendix to Husenbeth's *Emblems*, which gives German, French, Spanish, Greek, Scottish, and Sarum, in addition to those here printed; also to R. T. Hampson's *Medii Aevi Kalendarium*, a storehouse of many odds and ends, including calendars dating from the tenth to the fifteenth century.

For information in detail, the reader should consult Alban Butler's *Lives of the Saints* (in twelve volumes), Baring Gould's latest edition of the *Lives*, or any other standard work on the same subject.

CHAPTER XIX.

The Names of the Saints.

ARRANGED ALPHABETICALLY, WITH THEIR TRADITIONAL EMBLEMS.

S. Agapetus, M.	275	A lion at his feet.
S. Agatha, V.M.	251	Breasts in a dish, on a book, or in pincers; shears in her hand; chafing dish by her side.
S. Agnes, V.M.	304	Lamb on a book; lamb and palm; sword through her neck.
S. Aidan, B.C.	651	A stag; a lighted torch.
S. Alban, M.	303	Cross and square cap and sword; sun radiant above; book in hand.
S. Albinus, B.C.	549	Preaching from a pulpit; curing the blind.
S. Alphege, Archb. M.	1012	A chasuble full of stones; battle axe in hand.
S. Amphibalus, P.M.	303	Bound to a tree, and scourged.
S. Ambrose, B.C.D.	397	A scourge; a beehive; a tower; a dove near him.
S. Anastasia, V.M.	290	Burning at a stake.
S. Andrew, Ap. M.	64	A cross saltire; a V cross; two fishes in his hand.
S. Ann, the mother of Mary.	?	The child Mary by her side, learning to read; the holy infant in her arms also.
S. Anselm, B.C.D.	1109	A vision of our Lady and Child; holding a ship; or a Papal bull.
S. Anthony, Ab. C.	251	A crutched staff and bell; a pig with bell round its neck; a torch and bell; the devil in goat's form.
S. Anthony of Padua, C.	1231	The Holy Child seated on a book in his hand; preaching to fishes, etc.
SS. Aquila & Priscilla, MM.	?	Shoemakers' tools and tent.
S. Apollonia, V.M.	249	Pincers and tooth.
S. Athanasius, B.C.D.	372	An open book; two columns; in a boat.
S. Augustine of Hippo, B.C.D.	430	An inflamed heart; an arrow; an eagle; a child with spoon or shell by the sea shore; a light from heaven and the word *Veritas*.
S. Augustine of England, B.C.	604	Banner of the crucifixion; baptizing King Ethelbert.
S. Barbara, V.M.	306	A tower and palm; or chalice; or a monstrance; or peacock's feather, etc.
S. Barnabas, Ap.	?	S. Matthew's gospel in the hand; three stones; book and staff.
S. Bartholomew, Ap.	?	A flaying knife and a book; devil under his feet.
S. Basil, B.C.D.	379	Carrying a church; dove at his head; column of fire.

The Names of the Saints.   155

S. Bees, Abbs.	650	Holding a convent.
S. Beatrice, V.M	303	Holding a rope.
S. Bede, C.	735	Holding a pitcher of water; light from heaven.
S. Benedict, Ab.	543	A cup on a book with serpent; a raven; a pitcher; a ball of fire; a broken bell; asperges brush, etc.
S. Bennet Biscop, Ab.	690	Standing by river Tyne, two monasteries in sight.
S. Bernard, Ab. D.	1153	The instruments of the Passion; a white dog; a beehive; B. V. M. appearing.
S. Blaize, B.M.	304	Crozier and book; a wool comb; a pig's head; taking thorn from child's throat.
S. Boniface, B.M.*	755	Book pierced with sword; a scourge; beaten to death with club.
S. Botolph, Ab.	655	Church in hand.
S. Bridget (of Kildare).	523	A flame over head; casting out devil; a cow by her side.
S. Britius or Brice, B.C.	444	A child in his arms; burning coals in his hands.
S. Bruno, C.	1101	Crucifix flowering; star on breast; chalice and host in hand.
S. Catharine, V.M.	290	A wheel set with spikes; hailstones descending on her torturers; wheel broken; carried by angels.
S. Catharine of Siena, V.	1380	Crowned with thorns; espoused to Infant Saviour.
S. Cecilia, V.M.	220	An organ; a violin; a harp; a wreath of red roses; neck pierced with three wounds.
S. Chad, B.C.	672	Holding a branch; Lichfield Cathedral.
S. Charles Boromeo, B.C.	1584	Kneeling before altar; rope round his neck.
S. Chrysostom, B.C.D.	407	A beehive; chalice on Gospels.
S. Christina, V.M.	300	Pierced with three arrows; millstone round neck.
S. Christopher, M.	250	The Holy Child borne on the giant's shoulder; a lantern; in one example the Child has *three heads*.
S. Clare, Abbs.	1253	Blessed Sacrament in her hand; offering her heart to B. V. M.
S. Clement, Pope, M.	100	Double or triple cross; anchor; fountain; tiara.
S. Columba of Iona, Ab.	597	In a coracle; a white horse.
S. Columban, Ab.	615	In a bear's den; crucifix foliated.
S. Cornelius, Pope, M.	250	Horn and triple cross; cows around him.
SS. Crispin & Crispian, MM.	280	Shoemakers' tools; millstones.
SS. Cosmas & Damian, MM.	290	Surgical instruments; vases and arrows.
S. Cuthbert, B.C.	687	The head of S. Oswald; swans and otters; three loaves on table.
S Cyprian, B.M.	258	Gridiron and sword; books of magic burning.

* Winfred, born at Crediton, Archbishop of Maintz.

S. Cyril of Jerusalem, Abp. C.	386	A purse in his hand.
S. Cyril of Alexandria, B.C.	444	The B. V. M. appearing.
S. Damasus, Pope, C.	384	Holding a ring; a scroll with *Gloria Patri*; by a church door.
S. David, B.C.	544	A dove on the shoulder.
S. Denis or Dionysius, B.M.	272	Mitred head carried in the hands or on a book; tied to a tree.
S. Dominic, C.	1221	A lily; a star on his forehead; rosary in the hand.
S. Dorothy, V.M.	250?	Basket of fruit (and flowers); burning torch.
S. Dubritius, B.C.	550?	Holding two crosiers and archbishop's cross.
S. Dunstan, B.C.	988	The devil caught by pincers; a troop of angels; a covered cup.
S. Edith, V.	984	A "Royal" Nun; washing feet of poor.
S. Edmund, Abp.	1242	Child at his feet; B. V. M. giving him a ring.
S. Edmund, K.M.	870	Arrows piercing him; arrow and sceptre.
S. Edward, K.M.	1066	Dagger and cup; dagger and sceptre.
S. Edward, K.C.	979	A sceptre; a ring held in left hand; a purse hanging from right arm; S. John's Gospel.
S. Edwyn, K.M.	633	Three mitres and a chain.
S. Elizabeth.		Shown saluting the B. V. M.; holding S. J. B.
S. Eligius (Eloi), B.C.	665	Fetters on legs; hammer in hand.
S. Elizabeth of Hungary, IV.	1231	A triple crown; a basket of bread, and flagon of wine; roses in robe.
S. Erasmus, B.M.	303	A windlass (with entrails wound round it); ravens bringing bread.
S. Ethelburga, Abbs.	664	Instruments of the Passion.
S. Etheldreda, V. Abbs.	679	A crozier and crown of flowers; book and lily.
S. Ennrchus, B.C. ?	340?	A dove on the head.
S. Fabian, Pope, M.	250	A block at which he kneels; a dove; a sword; a club.
S. Faith, V.M.	350?	An iron bed; book; bundle of rods.
S. Felix of Nola, C.	266	Potsherds; chained in prison.
S. Francis of Assisi, C.	1226	A crown of thorns; the stigmata; a fiery chariot; preaching to birds.
S. Flavian, M.	380	Branded on forehead.
S. Gabriel, Archangel.		Sceptre and lily; shield with MR; lantern in right hand, mirror in left.
S. Genevieve, V.	512	A shepherdess spinning; a devil with bellows on her shoulder.
S. German, B.C.	448	Leading dragon with seven heads; trampling on Maximius.
S. George, M.	250?	A dragon slain by him with spear; banner of S. George; on horseback.
S. Gertrude, V.	664	Spinning; mice and rats round her; a loaf.

S. Gilbert, Abb. C.	1189	A church in hand.
S. Giles, Abb.	680?	Hind at his feet; arrow in breast.
S. Gregory, Thaumaturgus, B.C.	270	Devils driven out of a temple.
S. Gregory, Nazianzen, B.C.D.	389	Shown reading, *Wisdom* and *Chastity* appearing to him.
S. Gregory of Tours, B.C.	596	A fish; or reliquary in his hand.
S. Gregory the Great, P.C.D.	604	Double or triple cross and tiara; a vision of CHRIST in His Passion on the altar.
S. Gudule, V.	712	Lantern; twisted taper; a loom.
S. Helena, Emps.	328	The "True Cross;" Church of Jerusalem in her hand; double cross.
S. Hilda, V. Abbs.	680	Snakes.
S. Hilary of Poictiers, B.C.	368	An island with serpents; a child in a cradle; three books.
S. Hilary of Arles.	449	Dove over head.
S. Hubert, B.C.	727	A stag (on a book), a crucifix between its horns; hunting horn.
S. Hugh, B.C.	1200	Holy Child in the host; a swan.
S. Irenæus, B.M.	202	Lighted torch.
S. Ignatius, B.M.	108	In chains exposed to lions; heart with I.H.C.
S. Innocent, Pope.	417	Angel bringing a crown.
S. Ives, B.C.	650?	Episcopal habit.
S. James, Major, Ap. M.	44	Pilgrim's staff, shell, hat, and wallet; keys in hand.
S. James, Minor, Ap. M.	61?	Fuller's club; a saw; a toy windmill.
S. Januarius, B.M.	305	A heated oven; a vial of blood on book of Gospels.
S. Jerome, Card. D.	420	A cardinal's hat; a lion; an inkhorn; a scroll inscribed *Ciceronianus es*.
S. Joachim.	?	Basket with doves.
S. Joanna.	?	An ointment box; pitcher in a basket.
S. John Baptist.	30?	A lamb on book; a garment of camel's hair; a locust; a head on a dish.
S. John of Beverley, B.C.	721	By a shrine.
S. John Evangelist.	100?	A cup with serpent; an eagle; sword with serpent; a cauldron; a grave.
S. Joseph, the spouse.	?	A rod blossoming with lilies or almonds; a carpenter's square or tools.
S. Joseph of Arimathaea.	?	Box of ointment; a budding thorn staff.
S. Jude, Ap. M.	?	A boat; a club; an inverted cross; a halbert; a square; loaves and fish.
S. Julian, M.	313?	A stag; a ferry boat; an oar.
S. Kenelm, K.M.	819	A thorn tree, and light from heaven.
S. Kentigern (Mungo).	601?	A salmon with ring in gills; plough drawn by two deer.

S. Lambert, B.M.	709	Javelins; hot coals in robe.
S. Laurence, M.	258	Gridiron; palm and crucifix; as Deacon with censer.
S. Leodegar, B.M. (S. Leger).	678	Pickaxe or auger in hand.
S. Leo, Pope, C.	461	On horseback, Attila and soldiers kneeling.
S. Leonard, C.	520	An ox; chains; broken fetters; a vane.
S. Louis, K.C.	1270	Crown of thorns; lilies of France; three nails.
S. Lucy, V.M.	304	Eyes on a book, or dish; a lamp; sword through neck; holding three crowns; pincers; dragged by oxen.
S. Luke, Evangelist.	?	An ox; picture of B. V. M.
S. Machutus, B.C. (S. Malo).	630	Child at his feet; healing blind nobleman.
S. Magnus, B. ?	660	A bear under an apple tree.
S. Margaret, V.M.	306	A dragon chained; rising from dragon; a girdle; sheep.
S. Margaret, Qu. (Scot).	1093	A black cross; sceptre and book; shown visiting the sick.
S. Mark, Evangelist.	?	A lion; a fig tree; a cardinal's hat.
S. Martha, V.	?	A ladle; keys at girdle; asperges; dragon at feet.
S. Martin, B.C.	402	A beggar receiving half the saint's cloak, which he cuts with his sword.
The Blessed Virgin Mary.		The lily; the marigold; the crowned M.; the star; twelve stars; the *fleur-de-lys*; the ark of the covenant; the gate of heaven; the sun and moon; the rod of Jesse; the fountain; the garden enclosed; the tower of ivory; the city of GOD; the well of living waters; serpents beneath her feet.
S. Mary Magdalene, Pen.	?	A box of ointment; a skull; a book; long hair covering her.
S. Mary of Cleopas.	?	Four children bearing emblems—(1) a boat, (2) a toy mill, (3) a fish, (4) a cup.
S. Mary of Egypt, Pen.	321	Covered with long white hair, holding three loaves; death's head.
S. Matthias, Ap. M.	?	A halbert or lance; a stone; a sword held by the point; a carpenter's square.
S. Matthew, Ap. Evangelist.	?	An angel; a dolphin; a money bag; a battle axe; a square; a tiara.
S. Maurice, M.	280	In armour (often as a Moor); with banner of lion, or seven stars.
SS. Medard, & Geldard, BB.MM.	545	Two white doves (or three).
S. Michael, Archangel.		In armour; scales, with souls; or souls in one, millstone in other; piercing the devil; banner with dove; lance and shield.
S. Mildred, V. Abbs.	670	Holding Minster Abbey.

S. Milburg, V. Abbs.	664	Flock of wild swans.
S. Monica, Wid.	387	A handkerchief and open book; a tablet with I.H.S.; a monstrance.
S. Nicholas, B.C.	342	Three children (in tub); three golden balls (or six); three golden apples; or loaves; or purses; an anchor; a ship.
S. Nicomede, P.M.	90	Holding a spiked club.
S. Olave, K.M.	1030	Sceptre and sword; battle axe; halbert and loaf; a ladder.
S. Osyth, V.M.	870	Carrying her head cut off; a bunch of keys, and three loaves.
S. Oswald, K.M.	642	Sceptre and cross; a horn; a raven, with a ring in its beak, or a letter and a box of chrism.
S. Oswyn, K.M.	651	A spear; a spear and sceptre.
S. Ouen, Archb.	683	A coffin in a boat; a cross in the air.
S. Paternus, B.C.	565	A serpent.
S. Pancras, M.	304	A sword and stone.
S. Patrick, B.C.	464	Serpents at his feet; a fire before him; the "trefoil" or shamrock; a font.
S. Paul, Ap. M.	68	A sword (and book); three springs of water; two swords.
S. Paulinus, B.C.	431	Holding a church; a spade.
S. Perpetua, M.	203	A wild cow; a ladder guarded by dragon.
S. Petrock, C.	564	A box of relics.
S. Peter, Ap. M.	68	A key, or two keys, one gold and one silver; a cock crowing; an inverted cross.
S. Peter, M.	1252	Knife in his shoulder; in his head; writing *Credo* with his blood.
S. Philip, Ap. M.	?	A basket; two or three loaves and a cross; a spear and double cross; a knotted cross; devils and idols dispersed.
S. Polycarp, B.M.	166	A pile of wood in flames; stabbed and burned.
S. Prisca.	275	A lion (or two lions); an eagle; a sword.
S. Radegund, Queen.	587	Chain; two wolves; field of oats; crown, sceptre, and crozier.
S. Raphael, Archangel.		A staff; a wallet; a fish.
S. Remigins, B.C.	545	Carrying holy oils; birds feeding from hand; regarding the veil of Veronica; dove bringing him the chrism.
S. Richard, B.C.	1253	A plough; a chalice at his feet.
S. Rupert, B.C	718	A salt box; a church in hands.
S. Sampson, B.C.	565	The Cathedral of Dol in his hands.
S. Sebastian, M.	288	A bunch of arrows; the same piercing him; bound to a tree; holding a bow.
S. Sidwell, V.M.	740	A scythe; carrying her own head; a well by her.

S. Simon, Ap. M.	?	A fish (or two fishes); an oar; a fuller's bat; a saw.
S. Stephen, Deacon M.	34?	Stones in a napkin, in dalmatic or in hand, or one on the head.
S. Swithun, B.C.	969	A cross in right arm.
S. Sylvester, P.C.	335	Constantine being baptized; an ox; a double cross; a tiara; holding a chained dragon.
S. Symphorian, M.	270	A statue of Cybele.
S. Theobald, B.C.	1066	Episcopal vestments; in hermit's cell.
S. Thecla, V.M.	cent. 1	Lion; two serpents; globe of fire in hand.
S. Theodore, B.C.	613	Spearing a dragon; on horseback; crocodile.
S. Thomas, Ap. M.	?	A spear or lance; a square; an arrow; touching the sacred wounds.
S. Thomas à Becket, Abp. M.	1170	Pallium; archi-episcopal cross; sword through mitre, or across the back of his head; a battle axe; crosier.
S. Thomas Aquinas, C.D.	1274	A star, or sun on the breast; chalice and host; shown with wings.
S. Timothy, B.M.	97	A club and stones.
S. Urban, P.M.	230	Scourged at a stake; beheaded.
S. Ursula, V.M.	453	An arrow; a dove; a book; virgins beneath her mantle; ship.
S. Uriel, Archangel.		Holding a sword; a scroll; flames in left hand; at feet.
S. Valentine, M.	270	As Priest bearing sword; holding sun.
S. Vedast, B.C.	539	A wolf, with a goose in its mouth; or in a thicket.
S. Victor, M.	303	In chain mail; foot cut off; millstone and sword; holding a banner, and windmill.
S. Veronica, V.		The handkerchief with the SAVIOUR's Face.
S. Vincent, Deacon M.	304	An iron hook; a gridiron; a crow; a palm; a canoe in hand; book and dalmatic.
S. Vitus, B.M.	285	A cockatrice on book; a wolf; a lion; a fire.
S. Wenceslas, K.M.	938	In armour; reaping corn; coffin borne by angels.
S. William of York, B.C.	1154	An Archi-episcopal cross; lozenged shield.
S. William of Norwich, M.	1137	Crucified child; three nails in head; three held in right hand, and hammer in left.
S. Winifred, V.M.	650	Head carried in her hands.
S. Wilfrid, Archb. C.	709	Cathedral (of Ripon); idols falling down.
S. Winwallow, Abb.	529	Bell; fishes.
S. Wulstan, B.C.	1095	Crozier fixed in S. Edward the Confessor's tomb.

Besides the emblems here given there are many others attributed to the saints enumerated; as also there are many saints whose emblems are unknown, and emblems, the reference of which has been lost; so there are, unhappily, often found paintings and statues, so little distinctive or individual, that we can only accord them their position, and thankfully number them among All Saints.

CHAPTER XX.

The Nimbus.

THAT so familiar a sign of honour, and one so inseparably connected by long association with the glory of GOD, and the honour of His Saints, should be in its origin heathen, jars our sense of congruity, and shocks our feelings. Yet undoubtedly the Nimbus, or "Glory," is neither Christian, nor sacred, in so far as we use that term with relation to Divine religion.

It was employed by the artists of ancient Greece and Rome, and it is used to-day in the Temples of India. Didron (Vol. i., p. 41) gives a drawing of Maya, the Hindoo goddess, whose head is surrounded not only with a nimbus, but one which is distinctly *cruciform*.

Montfaucon (*Antiquité expliquée*, vol. i.) gives an example of an Apollo crowned with a circular rayed nimbus. Lucian says that the Syrian goddess had rays upon her head.

"Juno," says Virgil, "came down to earth *nimbo succincta*."

That a nebulous radiation, a shadowy light, surrounded Divine beings, was, beyond question, believed by the ancients; as indeed by some persons it is still held to be the fact that a certain faint light radiates from every living man, invisible it may be to the unenlightened, but seen by the illuminati. Be this as it may, the universal idea of the ancients was that the heavenly beings were enshrined in light, and when manifested to human eyes, were surrounded with rays or a bright cloud.

This surrounding cloud, is commonly called the aureole. So far from its being, as described by Mackenzie Walcott, "an *extended* nimbus," it is more exact to call the nimbus a *contracted* aureole.

The aureole cannot, I think, with any reason be considered a development of the nimbus, nor can the nimbus with absolute certainty be said to be an outgrowth of the aureole, that is to say, it did not definitely succeed and displace it.

Plate XXXV. shows the nimbus, both in its Pagan and Christian forms; and no one can fail to be struck with their similarity.

Mercury, Apollo (fig. 7), Ceres, Circe, and Medea, among others, are all shown with the orthodox circular nimbus in ancient art. I am inclined to think that the nimbus, aureole, glory, or whatever we prefer to call it, is pre-eminently the sign of power.

Hence it was given, not only to the beneficent and mild, but to the feared and hated "powers of the air." Even in Christian times, Satan has been so distinguished,* and, as is well known, the Roman Emperors were depicted with the nimbus.

Undoubtedly the *genesis* of the nimbus or aureole, was the belief that actual light surrounded persons of superhuman power; its *use* in Christian art has, I believe, arisen simply from a desire to mark out with more abundant honour or distinction those so decorated.

The head is crowned as the honourable member of the body, and therefore the nimbus surrounds it alone, as a sufficient mark of glory.

The *common* use of this sign dates from the fifth century, but it was never universal, nor need it be so now.

The form of the nimbus varies almost infinitely, and its decoration is of the most diverse character.

It is generally said that our LORD is always shown with a cruciform glory. This, like many other such statements, is more or less true, but not absolutely so, by any means. Sometimes the nimbus is omitted altogether, and even when used it is not always crossed.

It has been stated that the cross upon the nimbus is not a cross at all, but a triple ray showing the mystery of the Holy Trinity. This, I suppose, is owing to the fact that the common position of the head obviously prevents more than three of the four members being visible, so long, that is to say, as the nimbus is *behind* the head; but when (as in fig. 10, or fig. 8) the view is taken *from behind*, the cross is shown entire. The former of these two examples is from a picture by Fra Angelico, the latter from a wood carving in Amiens.

The Divine nimbus surrounding the head of the Almighty FATHER is sometimes square or lozenge shaped, and sometimes triangular.

Fig. 6 is from a Greek fresco of the seventeenth century.

Fig. 5 from a sixteenth century miniature.

Fig. 11 is also from a Greek fresco at Mount Athos.

The more usual method of depicting the nimbus of the Godhead in western art, is to employ a plain circular nimbus signed with the cross. This cross is mostly (fig. 3) plain with slightly extended ends, but often it is more ornate, and sometimes most intricately foliated.

Starting from a simple *fleur de lys* (fig. 2 *b.*), the cross became floriated, as (*a*) or (*c*); and in the later German school, such painters as Michael Wohlgemuth, Van Eyck, and Albert Dürer frequently elaborated the terminations of the cross, until they interlaced like the branches of a thorn bush.

Sometimes the simple circle of the nimbus had thin gold rays within it, and sometimes the rays passed the circle, as fig. 4.

A large proportion (an overwhelming majority, indeed) are shown in "true elevation," but sometimes they are in "perspective" (figs. 9, 10, 8).

---

* Possibly the satanic nimbus has a reference to 2 Corinthians xi. 14, where Satan is said to be sometimes "himself transformed into an angel of light"—noticeably in the Temptation of the LORD, when he sought to dazzle Him with the "glory of the world."

Some early examples are square, figs. 16 and 13, for instance, of the ninth century. It is asserted by some that these forms were employed for *living* persons, but there is no sufficient foundation for this theory.

Sometimes the nimbus was octagonal or polygonal, and sometimes hexagonal.

Fig. 14 is from a painting by Giotto, and represents "Poverty;" fig. 15 is from a fifteenth century MS., and surrounds the head of S. Joseph.

Often the circle of the nimbus is altogether absent, and light rays of gold surround the head; fig. 12, from a sixteenth century MS., has the rays in the form of a cross, but many others show a circle of radiating lines of equal length.

The nimbus, when shown to the Pelican, the Holy Dove, the Chalice, and the Agnus Dei is for the most part cruciform; but beyond this there is neither rule nor law to govern the representation.

Angels and saints are shown with every variety of nimbus. Sometimes the border is enriched, as fig. 17; sometimes jewelled, as fig. 18; and frequently within a double rim is the name of the saint portrayed, fig. 19.

The aureole, or larger glory, is either trefoiled, circular, quatrefoiled, or elliptical. It is either formed by clear and sharp containing lines, or it is of rays, or clouds.

Generally speaking, the aureole is confined to figures of the Blessed Trinity, our Redeemer, our Lady, or to the Chalice and Host.

There is, indeed, an early example of a saint (Martin) in Chartres Cathedral, but here it is the *soul* shown naked, and not the living body of the saint.

Fig. 1 will, perhaps, serve as a sufficient example of an aureole, formed by rays of light. It is given in Didron as from a sixteenth century window at Jouy, near Rheims.

Or that given below, from a sixteenth century miniature, is, perhaps, even a more pleasing one.

It is impossible to say all that could be said, or has been said, on the history, symbolism, and use of the glory in sacred art ; and, for my own part, I incline to the opinion that far too much has been said. Didron devotes 170 pages to the subject in the first volume of his *Iconography*, but neither his facts nor his theories are very conclusive. The article by Canon Venables in Smith's *Dictionary of Christian Antiquities* tells all that need be considered from the archaeological or historical point of view ; and beyond that, we may be content to say that the nimbus *may* be of any sort or kind or shape.

We should, of course, never put a cruciform or triple nimbus to a human being ; and if our picture is of mediaeval style we had better use the common circular form in all cases.

CHAPTER XXI.

The Heraldry of the Shield.

A FEW words are necessary on the subject of Heraldry *per se*, though it can here be possible to provide only the merest outlines of this grand science, without some knowledge of which neither architecture nor decoration can be intelligently studied or practised. History and art depend upon it, and no ancient building, secular or ecclesiastical, is entirely destitute of signs and marks, unerring records, unfailing keys to open out to us the past. So it is within our power, by the same means, to enlighten the future, and to give abiding interest to the works of the present. But to do this we must at least be preserved from the falsehoods and absurdities of mock heraldic insignia ; and whether we are striving to illustrate the days that are gone, or those in which we live, we must be sure that we are not perpetrating solecisms, and making sport for the well-taught or ill-natured. If we desire to paint or carve a shield, it must be a shield of the style in which we are working ; and if we employ the charges or figures or tints of blazonry, we must use them properly.

It is a safe rule to be careful and cautious in the employment of such things, lest we be either absolutely unmeaning or *too* meaning !

There is one sign, for instance, that should be marked with a danger signal—the *bendlet* or *baton sinister*, ✒. I once found to my horror that an enthusiastic decorator, in the innocence of his heart, had hung a shield so "abated" over the tomb of a nobleman, whose family *had* sprang from an illegitimate ancestor. Generally, I grant that the amateur herald is quite innocuous, so far as any disrespect to the dead is concerned, but the insult to the intelligence of the living is unpardonable, when they are called to sit opposite suspended shields with red crosses on blue grounds ; or when green and gold ermine, with unmeaning bars and pales and saltires are daubed across the escutcheons of some sleeping knight, whose slumbers might well be disturbed at such stupid interference.

The bare rudiments of heraldic science are at least within the reach of all ; and they may be summarised as follows :—

(*a*)

The shield has no special shape, but may vary indefinitely. (See the next Chapter.)

(*b*)

Whatever its shape it has the same constitution and parts. (See figs. 18 and 19, Plate XXXVII.). A is the *dexter* side, B is the *sinister ;* that is to say, right and left as they would be to the *wearer* of the shield.

C is the *Chief*, and D is the *Base*. E, the upper right quarter, is the *Dexter Chief*, and the opposite, F is the *Sinister Chief*. G is the *Middle Chief*. H the *Dexter Base*. I the *Sinister Base*, and K the *Middle Base*. L is the *Honour Point*, and M the *Fesse Point*, that is to say, the point at which a *fesse* would pass on a shield.

(c)

A shield may be divided or "parted" in six ways only.

Fig. 1, *per Pale*. When two coats of arms share a shield between them they are said to be impaled.

Fig. 2, *per Fesse*.

Figs. 3, 9, 10, and 11, *per Cross*, or *Quarterly*. If two coats are borne thus they are said to be *quartered*.

Fig. 4, *per Bend*, that is to say, on the line taken by a "bend" if it were used as a charge.

Fig. 5, *per Saltire*.

Fig. 6, *per Chevron*.

Besides these main divisions, there are, of course, the subsidiary ones of dividing an impaled half, as though it were a complete shield, and so with the quartered shield.

(d)

The whole surface of the shield is called the *Field*, and so of its parts we may say that the Chief, or the Bend, or the Fesse is a field, when we are further describing something placed or *charged* on it.

(e)

The Tinctures of Heraldry, shown by lines of shading where colour is not employed, comprise Two **Metals**—*Or* (gold) and *Argent* (silver or white). These are shown on fig. X. (F and G). Five **Colours**—*Azure* (blue), A, fig. 1. *Gules* (red), B, fig. 1. *Vert* (green), C, fig. 2. *Purpure* (purple), D, fig. 2; and *Sable* (black), E, fig. 6. These terms are commonly abbreviated thus: *or., arg., az., gu., vert., purp.*, and *sa*. Eight **Furs**, which are the following: (1) *Ermine*, black on white; (2) *Ermines*, white on black; (3) *Erminois*, black on gold; (4) *Pean*, gold on black; (5) *Vair*; (6) *Counter vair*; (7) *Potent*; (8) *Counter potent*. See shields, figs. 3, 4, 5, and 6, Plate XXXVI.

The lines and dots used to express the colours are not ancient, but they are extremely convenient.

The metals are said to take precedence of the colours. Any object shown in its natural colouring, as a flower, or ship, or sword, is described as *proper* (or *ppr.*).

The broad rule for the employment of these metals and colours is that a colour must *never* be placed on a colour, nor a metal on a metal. A shield may be *divided* per pale, per fesse, per cross, and so on, into red and blue, gold and silver, etc.; but a cross, or a chevron, or a bar of red must not be charged on a field of green, nor gold on silver, etc., etc.

There is one solitary exception to this rule, which is given on shield X., the arms of the Crusader Kings of Jerusalem; who, perchance to show that their kingdom was not of this world, ran counter to the laws of earthly blazonry, and charged five golden crosses on a field of silver.

(f)

The next point, perhaps, to describe is the nature of the **lines** or edges of the parts of a shield, or a charge upon it. The lines are either plain, or, if otherwise, are described as *(a) Engrailed*, or *(b) Invected*, or *(c) Wavy*, or *(d) Nebulée*, or *(e) Indented*, or *(f) Dancette*, or *(g) Embattled*, or *(h) Ragulée*, or *(i) Dovetailed*. See figs. 6, 7, 8, Plate XXXVI.

(g)

With these lines are formed the figures named the **ordinaries**. They are nine in number:

The *Chief*, i.e., the uppermost third of the shield. See the dexter side of shield 8, where there is a chief *az*.

The *Fesse*, also a third, but the middle third of the field. See shield 9, where there is on the dexter side a fesse azure on a field argent.

The *Bar*, which occupies the same position as the fesse, but is a fifth of the field instead of a third. See the sinister side of shield 9, a Bar gules.

The *Pale* occupies a third of the field vertically. See sinister side of shield 8, a Bar ragulée, purpure, on a field argent.

The *Cross*, shield 10, unless otherwise described, has both its members running to the extreme limits of the field, and each bar is one-fifth, or thereabouts, of the width, unless any object is "charged" upon the cross, when the width is one-*third*.

The *Bend* (shield 10) is formed by two diagonal lines, running through the centre upwards from the sinister to the dexter. On shield 17 the Bend is shown *cotised*, i.e., flanked by two of its lesser diminutives.

A *Riband* is a cotise, couped or cut off at each end. Shield 16, a riband *az*. on a field *arg*.

The *Saltire* (see sinister side of shield 9). The members are of the same width as the cross or the bend.

The *Pile*, a wedge-shaped inverted triangle. See shield 18.

(h)

The next group of charges consists of the **Roundles**. These are the *Bezant (or.)*, the *Plate (arg.)*, the *Hurte (az.)*, the *Torteau (gu.)*, the *Pellet (sa.)*, the *Pomme (vert)*, and the *Fountain* (of wavy stripes, *az*. and *arg*.). These are shown on shields 15 and 15a.

(i)

The **diminutives** of the ordinaries are:

The *Fillet*, one-fourth of the *Chief*. Always shown at the lowest portion of the space which would be occupied by the chief itself (see shield 12, sinister side).

The *Closet* is one-half, the *Barrulet*, one-quarter of the *Bar*.

The *Pallet* is one-half, and the *Endorse* one-quarter of the *Pale*. See shield 13, where a Pallet is "endorsed."

The *Bendlet* is one-half, and the *Cotise* one-quarter of the Bend (see shields 13 and 17).

The *Chevronel* is one-half of the *Chevron* (see shield 20).

(*k*)

The **subordinaries** are fourteen in number:

The *Canton*, a square at the dexter chief corner. This always surmounts a *bordure*, occupying one-ninth of the shield's area (see No. 20).

The *Gyron* is half the first quarter of the shield (see shield 18): if the field is divided by a continuation of its lines, it is said to be gyronny.

The *Inescutcheon*, called also the shield of pretence, is a small shield on a shield (see 19 *a*).

The *Orle* (see shield 12) is a narrow border within the shield, and not on its outer edges. In this example, the shield being parti per pale, only half the orle is shown.

The *Tressure* (see shield 13) is a double orle with a *fleur de lys* enrichment. Here too, only half is shown.

The *Lozenge* (see shield 10).

The *Fusil* is the same, but elongated. ◊

The *Mascle* (see shield 10) is a lozenge voided, and the *Rustre* voided with a circular piercing.

The *Billet* is a rectangular oblong. See shield 19 (*a*).

The *Label* (see shield 11) is a riband having three, four, or five short "tags" depending from it.

The *Bordure* (see shield 18) is ordinarily one fifth of the width of the shield, though it is sometimes in old examples more, and sometimes much *less*, than this proportion.

The *Flanch* (*a*), called also a *Flasque* (*b*), if flat and narrow, is only used in pairs, and is formed by a curved line bowed towards the centre of the shield (see shield 14).

The *Frette* (see shield 11) is an interlaced figure, which is sometimes extended and multiplied till it covers the whole field, which is then described as fretty or frettée.

With these elementary instructions I fear my readers must rest content, or rather I trust they will *not*, but will pursue the study of Heraldry in some manual, of standard authority. Sufficient has been here set down, at least, to show the broad outlines of the method in which shields are to be treated, and probably a few pitfalls will be thereby avoided.

Nothing has been said about the figures or charges of animate and inanimate objects—lions, stags, roses, swords, and a multitude of other things. I would ask my readers by no means to rest satisfied with the information here provided, but to be assured that it is only the impossibility of the task that prevents my including in this book, a full and particular account of all that is, for want of space, omitted.

A note, however, as to light and shade: the light is supposed to fall on a shield from the dexter side, and from above, consequently an ordinary, or a charge, or a figure will always be "shaded," as the cross here shown, by the employment of a thicker line to the right and below.

A word, too, should be added on Heraldry, strictly ecclesiastical or sacred.

As has been already noticed, the Blessed Trinity, the Passion of our LORD, the Blessed Sacrament, and many of the saints, are credited with armorial bearings—these will be found described in their proper place; but, besides these, the various dioceses have their shields of arms, which the bishops wear; and if they have arms they are entitled to impale them with those of the diocese: the shield may also be surmounted with a mitre.

CHAPTER XXII.

The Form of the Shield.

SHIELDS are the commonest and most convenient vehicles for emblems, and clearly came from the battlefield and the tilting yard into the Church, and were intended, no doubt, to show that the champions of the Church militant had their cognizances and achievements, as well as the warriors of the world. Hence we see that from the font to the altar, from floor to roof, the Churches of the middle ages were filled with shields. So closely indeed did the shield ecclesiastical imitate the secular, that it was often hung up by its strap, and even had its dexter side notched with the spear rest!

In nearly every case the emblems, or "trophies," of the Passion are borne on shields; as also our LORD'S name, the Chalice and Host, and His Sacred Heart appear as His "Arms."

The conflict of His last dread fight upon the Cross was even spoken of as a tilting with His enemies, for, said an old writer thereon, "JESUS jousted well" when He received the spear thrust.

Not only our Blessed LORD, but His Apostles and Saints, too, bore shields of arms, or rather were credited with them, in the middle ages; some evidently apposite, but others (see, for instance, the shield of S. Nicholas), the purest apings of secular blazonry. Yet one cannot but sympathize with the pious feelings that made men place the saintly conflict on a knightly level; and if S. Paul thought it not unseemly to describe and symbolize the whole armour of GOD, even down to the shoes, there is nothing in itself either profane or undignified in giving the triumphant leaders in the war, their full insignia, as captains and officers in the saintly band.

The shape of the shield varied greatly, and on Plate XXIX.* thirty-one old shields are figured, from which it will be seen how gradually the simply curved triangle developed until it became fantastically crimped and scalloped in the fifteenth and sixteenth centuries.

The Early Norman shields were very long and tapering, as fig. 2, but if not concurrently with this form, at least in close succession, the short and equilateral shield, fig. 1, appeared. Sometimes the top edge was bowed upward, and sometimes downward, sometimes it was straight, as here drawn. In the thirteenth century little change took place in the general outline, though the proportion varied with the individual fancy of the wearer, or the mode of the day.

In the fourteenth century the tendency towards flowing lines in architecture,

---

* Repeated here for ease in reference to the Numbers.

The Form of the Shield.

and richness in ornamental detail, affected the shield both in use and representation. Fig. 5, of 1325, and fig. 4 (the shield of John of Gaunt), 1399, may stand as good examples of early departures from the severer forms. Not only did the outlines become more indented, but the surface was corrugated, rising often to three or more ridges on the face. So, too, the edges turned over, and were often floriated. See figs. 18, 21, and 25. This last is the shield of Henry V., when Prince of Wales, about 1410. Fig. 21 is from the Chantry Chapel of Abbot Ramrydge, of S. Albans. Fig. 23 is the latest example of all, being a shield of Henry VII., bearing his monogram.

Figs. 10, 11, 12, 22, are Flemish or German, and are copied from brasses and wood-carving. They are all of them late fifteenth century in style. It will be noticed that the bottom has here entirely lost its pointed shape, and become blunt and round; but fig. 28, also German, preserves the point.

Nearly all the remaining shields on Plate XXIX. are of the fifteenth century. Figs. 30 and 31, of unusual shape, are from wood-carving in Abbotsham Church, near Westward Ho. Fig. 17 is from a bench end in Mullion Church, and fig. 14 from Camborne, in Cornwall.

This collection of shields is by no means full or exhaustive, but perhaps it is ample enough to show the main varieties.

The positions occupied by shields in old Churches are sufficiently well known, but it may be noticed that the font was almost the *chief*: a very large proportion of fonts from the thirteenth century onwards were panelled on all eight sides; of these often the whole, and nearly always the alternate panels, were filled with shields.

The common course of the modern decorator is naturally to take the readiest way; and as a shield helps easily, he hangs his shields on the wall freely, though indeed, as often as not, he forgets to *hang* them, and simply *sticks* them on.

It will generally be found that in old work, shields were either *hung* by their band on to a bough or scroll, or *held* by angels, as in the hammer beam roofs, or *wedged* into a panel, or quatrefoil, or spandrel: in any case *safe* from falling.

So, tempting and legitimate as the use of shields may be, they must not be taken merely because they are always at hand, for only when suitably placed can they look comfortable and comely.

CHAPTER XXIII.

The Arms and Emblems of the Saints.

AMONG the many emblems of the saints there are, as has been already said, some which have acquired by long usage the position of heraldic insignia; and when shown on shields they are accounted as true escutcheons of "arms."

Several of these are blazoned in ancient MSS., or are to be found carved and painted on fonts and screens and windows in various parts of England.

The better known of these are figured on XXXVIII. and following Plates, but besides the actual "arms" I have added a few of the more "heraldic" emblems which can fairly be charged on shields, when these are used decoratively, in conjunction with figures of the saints; or in any other position suitable and significant. No *colours* can, however, be given to these latter as proper to them, and therefore there is a free choice, only restricted by the laws of heraldry.

ON PLATE XXXVIII.

S. PETER. ARMS, *gu.* two keys in saltire *arg.*

Emblems, a reversed cross, with two keys in saltire; or a patriarchal cross with the same.

S. PAUL. ARMS, *gu.* two swords in saltire *arg.*, hilted *or.*

Emblems, a book, inscribed, *Spiritus gladius*, surmounting a sword; or three "fountains."

S. ANDREW. ARMS, *gu.* a cross saltire *arg.*

Emblems, a V-shaped frame of wood; and two fishes.

S. JAMES THE GREAT. ARMS, *az.* three scallops *or.* two and one.

Emblems, a wallet and staff; or a pilgrim's hat and staff.

ON PLATE XXXIX.

S. JOHN EVANGELIST. ARMS, *az.* a Prester John, mitred, seated on an altar-tomb, right hand extended, an orb in left, a sword in his mouth, all *ppr.*; or as shown here, with a book in left hand, and right hand raised in benediction.

Emblems, a serpent issuing from a chalice; or a serpent entwined round a sword; or an eagle issuing from a cauldron.

S. THOMAS, a carpenter's square and a spear.

S. BARTHOLOMEW. ARMS, *gu.* three flaying knives, erect in fesse *arg.*, handled *or.*

Emblem, a knife on an open book.

S. PHILIP. A basket; or a tall cross and three loaves; or a patriarchal cross and a spear.

S. JAMES THE LESS. A saw; or a fuller's club.

On Plate XL.

S. JUDE. A ship; or a square and a boat-hook; or a reversed cross.

S. MATTHEW. Three purses; or a battle axe; or a T cross.

S. SIMON. A closed book and a fish; or a saw and an oar crossed.

S. MATTHIAS. A scimitar and a closed book.

S. BARNABAS. The Gospel of S. Matthew and three stones.

S. JOHN BAPTIST. The lamb and book.

S. JOSEPH. The lily, surmounting a carpenter's square.

On Plate XLI.

S. AGATHA. Fig. 1. Two breasts in a dish, and an eye in a pair of pincers.

S. AGNES. Fig. 2. A lamb upon a book.

S. AIDAN. Fig. 3. A stag.

S. ALBAN. Fig. 4. ARMS, az. a saltire or.
Emblems, a tall cross, palm and sword, and a priest's cap, fig. 4a.

S. ALBERT, King and Confessor. Fig. 5. ARMS, gu. a bezant between three crowns or.

S. ALBINE. Fig. 6. ARMS, az. a cross potent arg. between four letters A or.

S. ALBRIGHT. Fig. 7. ARMS, or. five chevronels az.

S. AMPHIBALUS. Fig. 8. ARMS, quarterly gu. and or. Four lions rampant counterchanged.

S. AMBROSE. Fig. 9. A bee-hive surmounting two scourges.

S. ANSELM. Fig. 10. ARMS, arg., gouttée de sang; a cross patée gu; or fig. 10a. arg., a cross sa., between twelve gouttes gu.

On Plate XLII.

S. ANTHONY. Fig. 1. ARMS, or. a tau cross az.; (1a) two bells and a pilgrim's staff.

S. ATHANASIUS. Fig. 2. An open book between two columns.

S. AUGUSTINE of Hippo. Fig. 3. A flaming heart transfixed by two arrows; fig. 3a., a light from heaven shining on the word veritas.

S. AUGUSTINE of Canterbury. Fig. 4. ARMS, sa. a cross arg.; in the dexter canton a pastoral staff erect, or. ensigned with cross patée arg., surmounted by a pall or.; in the sinister canton a lily slipped arg.; fig. 4a. arg. on a base gu., a font az., a naked man crowned or., issuant therefrom, inscribed, Ethelbert; fig. 4b. sa. a cross arg.

S. BARBARA. Fig. 5. A tower, with a chalice and host in a window thereof.

VEN. BEDE. Fig. 6. A pitcher, with a light from heaven.

S. BENEDICT. Fig. 7. A cup (with a dragon issuant), broken, and standing on a book.

S. BERNARD. Fig. 8. Three mitres on a book.

On Plate XLII.*

S. BLAISE. Fig. 1. A candle and two wool combs.

S. BONIFACE. Fig. 2. A book transfixed by a sword.

S. CATHARINE. Fig. 3. ARMS, *az.* a spiked wheel *arg.*

(Also

S. MARTIN. ARMS, *gu.* a catharine wheel *or.)*

S. BRIDGET. Fig. 4. A bunch of wheat ears.

S. CECILIA. Fig. 5. A harp.

S. CLARE. Fig. 6. A "Monstrance."

S. CHRYSOSTOM. Fig. 7. A chalice surmounting the Gospels.

S. CHAD. Fig. 8. ARMS, per pale, *gu.* and *arg.* a cross potent in fesse, between four crosses patées, all counter changed.

S. CLEMENT. Fig. 9. ARMS, *az.* an anchor in pale *or.*

S. CUTHBERT. Fig. 10. ARMS, *az.* a cross fleurée, *or.* between four lions rampant *arg.*

S. COMYN. Fig. 11. ARMS, *or.* nine torteaux 3, 3, and 3.

S. CRISPIN. Fig. 12. An awl and hammer crossed.

On Plate XLIII.

S. CYPRIAN. Fig. 1. A sword and a gridiron.

S. CYRIL. Fig. 2. A purse.

S. DENYS. Fig. 3. ARMS, *gu.* a cross fleurée *arg.*; another, *az.* a cross *arg.*; another, *gu.* a cross *arg.*, charged with a lion couchant gardant *az.*, mitred *or.*

S. DYONISIUS. Fig. 4. ARMS, *gu.* a cross *arg.* between four lions rampant.

S. DOMINIC. Fig. 5. ARMS, per chevron *sa.* and *arg.*; over all a crucifix *ppr.*

S. DUBRITIUS. Fig. 6. ARMS, *az.* a mitre transfixed by an archiepiscopal cross in pale, and two pastoral staves in saltire *or.*

S. DUNSTAN. Fig. 7. ARMS, *gu.* a covered cup *or.*

S. EDMUND, K.M. Fig. 8. ARMS, *az.* three crowns, two and one, *or.*; fig. 8*a. az.* a crown pierced with two arrows in saltire *or.*

S. EDMUND of Abingdon. Fig. 9. ARMS, *or.* a cross patonce *gu.*, between four Cornish choughs, *ppr.*; another, *gu.* a cross patonce *or.* between four sea-pies, *ppr.* (*sa.* winged *arg.*)

S. EDWARD CONF. Fig. 10. ARMS, *az.* a cross patonce between five martlets *or.*

On Plate XLIV.

S. EDWARD, K.M. Fig. 1. A cup and dagger. ARMS (Plate XLIII., fig. 11), *az.* a cross patée between four crowns, *or.*

S. EDWYN. Fig. 2. ARMS, *az.* a chain in chevron, with a ring on dexter, a horse lock on sinister between three mitres, all *or.*

S. ERKENWALD. Fig. 3. ARMS, *az.* a saltire *arg.* between two mitres in pale, and two crowns in fesse.

S. ERASMUS. Fig. 4. A windlass.

S. ETHELBERT. Fig. 5. ARMS, *gu.* three besants, two and one. 1, charged a lion rampant, *arg.*; 2, a dragon salient, *arg.*; 3, a demi-king, vested and crowned, *ppr.*

S. ETHELBERT II. Fig. 6. ARMS, *gu.* three crowns, two and one, *or.*

S. ETHELDREDA. Fig. 7. Arms as above.

S. ETHELRED. Fig. 8. ARMS, *az.* a cross potent fitchée *or.*

S. FAITH. ARMS, *gu.* a Trinity, *or.* This shield is not figured, as it is found on Plate XV., fig. 8.

S. FRIDESWIDE. Fig. 9. ARMS, *sa.* a fesse enhanced *arg.*, in chief three ladies' heads couped below the shoulders, *ppr.*, veiled *arg.* crowned *or.*, in base an ox *arg.* passing a ford *ppr.*

S. GEORGE. Fig. 10. ARMS, *gu.* seven mascles *or.* placed 3, 3, and 1. Another *arg.* a cross *gu.*

S. GILBERT. Fig. 11. ARMS, barry of six, *arg.* and *az.* over all a pilgrim's staff in bend *or.*

S. GERTRUDE. Fig. 12. A loaf of bread and three mice.

ON PLATE XLV.

S. GREGORY THE GREAT. Fig. 1. ARMS, *or.* three bendlets *gu.* on a chief, *or.* two lions counter rampant, supporting a torteau inscribed IHS. all *gu.*

S. HELEN. Fig. 2. A double cross with a hammer, and a nail over a cup.

S. HILDA. Fig. 3. ARMS. *az.* three snakes coiled, 2 and 1, *or.*

S. HUBERT. Fig. 4. A hunter's horn and a book.

S. HUGH. Fig. 5. ARMS, *az.* a saltire *erm.* between four *fleur de lys*, *or.* Another, fig. 5*a.* *vert.* a swan *arg.* drinking from a well *or.*

S. JEROME. Fig. 6. ARMS, *az.*, a cross potent fitchée *or.*

S. JOHN OF BEVERLEY. Fig. 7. ARMS, *arg.* a crown transfixed by a pastoral staff, *sa.* within a border of the last semée of Bezants.

S. JULIAN. Fig. 8. ARMS, *arg.* a cross crosslet in saltire *sa.*

S. LAURENCE. Fig. 9. ARMS, *arg.* a gridiron *sa.*

S. LEONARD. Fig. 10. A book surrounded by a chain.

S. LUCY. Fig. 11. A sword and palm crossed in saltire, a lamp and a book with two eyes upon it.

ON PLATE XLVI.

S. IGNATIUS, B.M. Fig. 1. A heart inscribed all over with IHS in gold.

S. LOUIS. Fig. 2. A crown of thorns crossed by two sceptres. The three nails in centre of wreath.

ARMS, fig. 2*a.* *az.* semée of *fleur de lys*, *or.*

S. MARGARET OF HUNGARY. Fig. 3. A royal crown with a lily growing through it.

S. KATHARINE OF SIENNA. Fig. 4. A heart enflamed, with a crucifix springing from it.

S. MAGNUS. Fig. 5. A pastoral staff with serpents entwined around it.

S. MARTHA. Fig. 6. A dragon pierced by a crucifix.

S. MARGARET OF SCOTLAND. Fig. 7. A black cross.

S. MAWR. Fig. 8. A spade surmounted by a pair of scales.

S. MARY MAGDALENE. Fig. 9. A skull on a book, with the legend *multum amavit*.

S. QUENTIN. Fig. 10. A red heart with a white cross upon it.

S. THOMAS AQUINAS. Fig. 11. The sacred monogram surrounded by the sun.

On Plate XLVII.

S. MARGARET. Fig. 1. A chained dragon.

S. MAURICE. Fig. 2. ARMS, *gu.* a cross and bordure *or.* Fig. 2*a. or.* à lion rampant *gu.*

S. MICHAEL. Fig. 3. ARMS, *arg.* a cross pommée *gu.*

S. MILDRED. Fig. 4. ARMS, *gu.* in fesse pt. a bell *arg.* with an orle of garbs *or.*

S. NICHOLAS. Fig. 5. ARMS, *Ermine*, a chief quarterly *or.* and *gu.*

Fig. 5*a.* Three golden balls on a book.

S. OLAVE. Fig. 6. A sceptre and sword crossed in saltire.

S. OSMUND. Fig. 7. ARMS, *or.* a saltire *sa.*

S. OSWALD. Fig. 8. ARMS, *az.* a cross patée, *or.* between three lions rampant, *arg.*

Another, *gu.* a cross fleurée *or.*

Another, per pale *or* and *gu.*

S. OSYTH. Fig. 9. ARMS, *or.* three crowns, two and one *gu.*

(S OSWYN. The same, but *az* and *or.*)

S. PATRICK. Fig 10. ARMS, *arg.* a saltire *gu.*

On Plate XLVIII.

S. PERPETUA. Fig. 1. A ladder with a dragon at the foot.

S. PRISCA. Fig. 2. An eagle.

S. RICHARD. Fig. 3. ARMS, *Ermine*, a pile *gu.*

S. REMIGIUS. Fig. 4. The kerchief of Veronica.

S. SEBASTIAN. Fig. 5. ARMS, *arg.* parti per pale ; in dexter seven crosses *gu.* in sinister, three arrows in pale points up, *az.*

S. STEPHEN. Fig. 6. A dalmatic with five stones upon it.

S. SYLVESTER. Fig. 7. A papal tiara surmounting a patriarchal cross.

S. THOMAS A BECKET. Fig. 8. ARMS, *arg.* three Cornish choughs *ppr.* two and one.

Fig. 8a. A mitre transfixed crosswise with a sword.
S. URSULA. Fig. 9. ARMS, *az.* semée of arrows, *or.* points in base, feathered *arg.*
S. VINCENT. Fig. 10. A spiked gridiron.
S. WILFRED. Fig. 11. ARMS, *az.* three estoiles *or.*, two and one.

CHAPTER XXIV.

The Arms of the English Bishoprics.

Very frequently we find in old churches (other than cathedrals) the arms of the diocese, either in conjunction with the arms of the patron, or used independently. It appeared, therefore, that it would not be an inappropriate supplement to saintly heraldry, to give the various arms of the English sees. They are therefore figured on Plates XLIX. and L.

On Plate XLIX.

Fig. 1. CANTERBURY.

az. an archi-episcopal staff in pale *or.* ensigned with a cross patée *arg.*, surmounted of a pall *arg.* charged with four crosses formée-fitchée, *sa.* edged and fringed *or.*

Fig. 2. YORK.

gu. two keys in saltire *arg.* in chief a royal crown *or.* (This crown is described as *imperial* by Boutell.)

The arms of York were formerly the same as those of Canterbury, but were changed in the reign of Henry VIII. to their present form.

Fig. 3. LONDON.

gu. two swords in saltire *arg.* pommelled *or.*

Fig. 4. BANGOR.

gu. a bend *or.* gouttée de poix, between two mullets pierced *arg.*

Fig. 5. WINCHESTER.

gu. two keys addorsed in bend sinister, the upper *arg.* the lower *or.*, a sword interposed between them *arg.* pommelled *or.*

Fig. 6. DURHAM.

az. a cross between four lions rampant *or.* Note that the mitre (when shown) is encircled by a ducal coronet.

Fig. 7. CHICHESTER.

az. a Prester John sitting on an altar tomb, a mound in the left hand, the right extended, all *or ;* a linen mitre on his head, and a sword in his mouth *ppr.*

Fig. 8. ELY.

gu. three ducal crowns, two and one *or.*

Fig. 9. EXETER.

gu. a sword in pale *ppr.* hilt *or.* surmounting two keys in saltire *or.*

Fig. 10. LLANDAFF.

sa. two croziers in saltire, *or.* and *arg.*, on a chief *az.* three mitres, labelled, *or.*

Arms of English Sees.

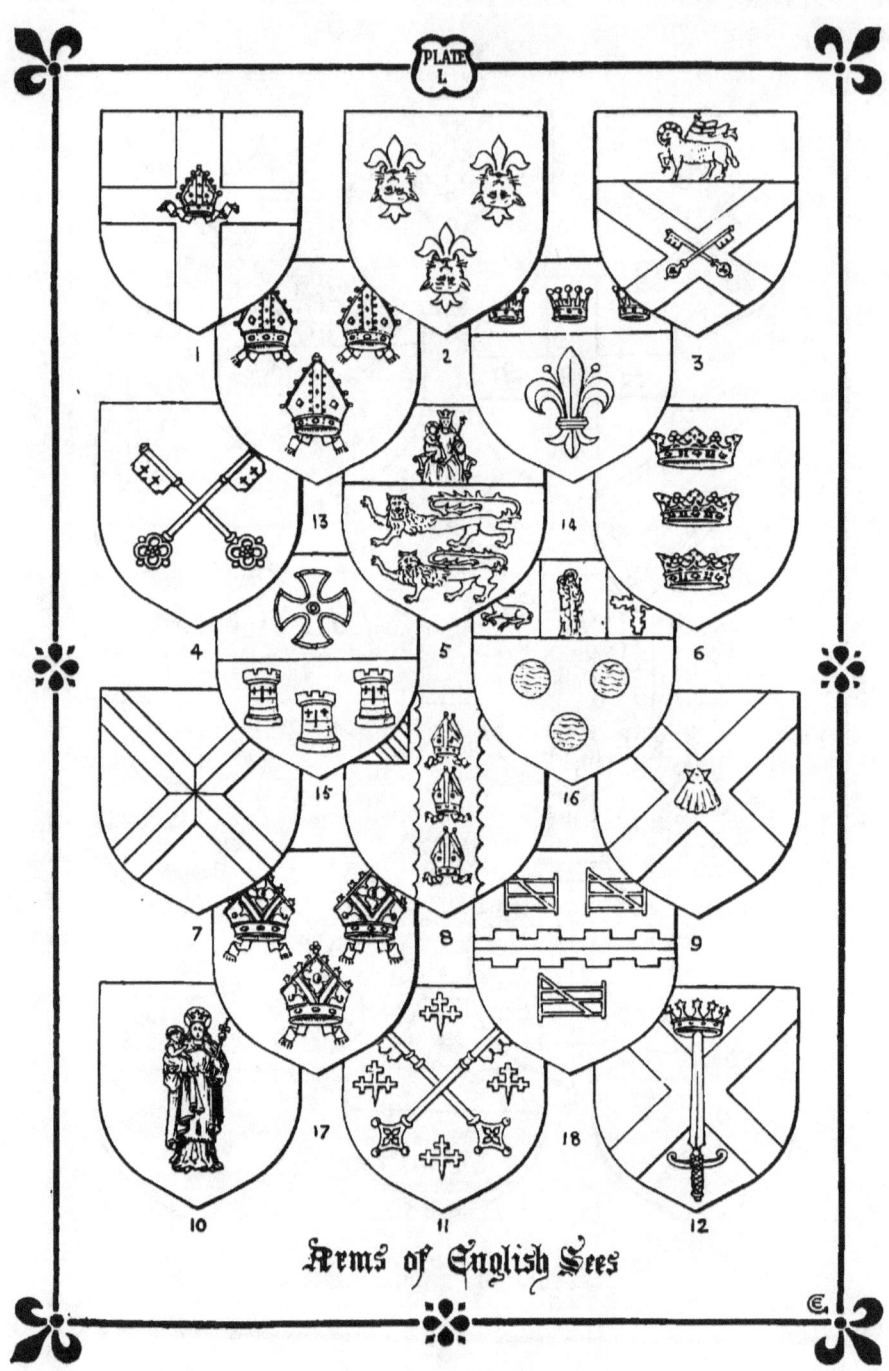

Arms of English Sees

The Arms of the English Bishoprics.

Fig. 11. OXFORD.

sa. a fesse *arg.* ; in chief three ladies, from the waist, heads affronté arrayed and veiled *arg.* crowned *or.* ; in base an ox *arg.* crossing a ford *ppr.*

Fig. 12. LIVERPOOL.

arg. an eagle with wings expanded *sa.* beaked *or.* resting its dexter claw on an ink-horn,*ppr.* a chief per pale, *az.* and *gu.* charged on dexter, an open book *or.* inscribed "Thy word is truth" *sa.* ; on sinister, a ship, or lymphad, *or.*

Fig. 13. S. DAVIDS.

sa. on a cross *or.* five cinqfoils *sa.*

Fig. 14. WESTMINSTER (Deanery).

az. a cross patonce between five martlets *or.* ; on a chief *or.* between two roses *gu.* a pale charged with the arms of modern France, (*az.* 3 *fleur de lys or.*) and England (*gu.* three leopards passant gardant *or.*).

Fig. 15. SODOR AND MAN.

arg. the Blessed Virgin on three ascents standing with arms extended between two pillars, on the dexter a church, in base the ancient arms of Man on an inescutcheon. (*gu.* three legs armed *ppr.* conjoined in the fesse point at the thighs flexed in a triangle, garnished and spurred *or.*)

Fig. 16. WORCESTER.

arg. ten torteaux in pile.

Fig. 17. LICHFIELD.

Parti per pale *gu.* and *arg.* a cross potent quadrate, between four crossslets-patées, all counterchanged.

(Note, Burke describes these crosslets as *gu.* and *or.* instead *gu.* and *arg.*)

Fig. 18. TRURO.

arg. on a saltire *gu.* a key, wards up, surmounted by a sword hilt up, in saltire, *or.* in base a *fleur de lys sa.* all within a bordure of Cornwall (*sa.* fifteen bezants).

On Plate L.

Fig 1. CARLISLE.

arg. on a cross *sa.* a mitre labelled *or.*

Fig. 2. HEREFORD.

gu. three leopards heads reversed, jessant of *fleur de lys or.*

Fig 3. RIPON.

arg. on a saltire *gu.* two keys in saltire, wards up *or.* on a chief *gu.* an Agnus Dei *ppr.*

Fig. 4. GLOUCESTER.

az two keys in saltire, wards up *or.*

Fig. 5. LINCOLN.

gu. two lions passant gardant *or.* on a chief the Blessed Virgin and Child, seated, crowned, and sceptred *or.*

Fig. 6. BRISTOL.

sa. three ducal crowns in pale *or.*

Fig. 7. (BATH AND) WELLS.
az. a saltire quarterly quartered, *or.* and *arg.* (These arms are those of *Wells* only.)

Fig. 8. MANCHESTER.
or. on a pale engrailed *gu.* three mitres labelled *or.* on a canton *gu.* three bendlets enhanced *arg.*

Fig. 9. ROCHESTER.
arg. on a saltire *gu.* an escallop *or.*

Fig. 10. SALISBURY.
az. the Blessed Virgin and Child crowned and sceptred all *or.*

Fig. 11. PETERBOROUGH.
gu. two keys in saltire between four cross crosslets fitchées *or.*

Fig. 12. S. ALBANS.
az. a saltire *or.* surmounted in pale by a sword *ppr.* hilted *or.* point up, towards a celestial crown in chief *or.*

Fig. 13. CHESTER.
gu. three mitres labelled, *or.*

Fig. 14. WAKEFIELD.
No arms granted.

Fig. 15. NEWCASTLE.
Per fesse, *az.* and *gu.* in chief S. Cuthbert's Cross *or.* in base three castles, two and one *arg.*

Fig. 16. SOUTHWELL.
sa. three fountains *ppr.* a chief paly of three, the first *or.* a stag, couchant, *ppr.* the second *gu.* our Lady and Child, *ppr.* the third *or.* two staves (coupled in cross) raguly, *vert.*

Fig. 17. NORWICH.
az. three mitres labelled *or.*

Fig. 18. SOUTHWARK.
No arms granted.

✠

CHAPTER XXV.

Crowns.

IN the days of "No cross, no crown" book-markers, the form familiar to our childish eyes was a spiked ring, either plain, or garnished with stars. This served all purposes, and, with the exception of the one surmounting the Royal arms, was the only form with which we were acquainted. Possibly, had we looked about us, our own Parish Church provided better examples, either in a stray pane of a dusty window, or on a half obliterated tile beneath the matting of the floor. But, speaking generally, the many beautiful shapes of the mediaeval crowns and coronets were unknown; consequently, in the early Church restorations, and the revival of symbolic decoration, a crown was a crown, and there the matter ended.

Nowadays we are better informed, and it may be that some of the examples here collected are so well known that they are almost superfluous; but it appeared to me that it would be well to put together on Plate LI. as many old examples possible, ranging from the days of the Conquest to the sixteenth century.

A few more specimens will be found on other plates, but the thirty-four figured here, form a fairly complete series. Fig. 1 is the crown of William the Conqueror, taken from his seal; fig. 2 that of Henry III., as shown on his tomb; fig. 3 is that of Edward II. at Gloucester; fig. 4, the crown of William Rufus; fig. 5, that of Queen Eleanor, wife of Henry II.; fig. 6, King Stephen; fig. 7, Henry II.; fig. 8, 1418, the coronet of Sir E. de Thorpe, from his brass; fig. 9 and fig. 15, crowns of Edward IV.; fig. 10, 1430, Margaret of Anjou; fig. 11 is a fifteenth century example, exact date unknown; fig. 12, a very rich coronet, is from the monument of the Countess of Richmond, 1509; figs. 13, 14, and 26 are all fifteenth century examples; fig. 15, the crown from the arms of Edward IV., 1480; fig. 16, from the brass of Sir Thomas Bromflete, 1430; fig. 17, from a German brass, 1457; fig. 18, a French example from Viollet le Duc's *Dictionaire du Mobilier*, date uncertain; fig. 19* is, perhaps, the most beautiful example of alternate *fleur de lys* and lofty crosses; figs. 20 and 22 are further examples from Viollet le Duc's book; fig. 21, from a painting of Martin Schöngauer about 1500; fig. 23 is from stained glass; fig. 24 is the popular "Martyr's Crown;" fig. 25 and 28 are Arundel coronets; fig. 27 is from the figure of Edward the Confessor in the Malvern window; fig. 30 is taken from the brass of King Eric of Denmark at Ringstead, and its date is 1319; figs. 31, 32, and 34 are from stained glass of the fifteenth century.

* From the Chantry of Abbot Wheatamstede, S. Albans.

With regard to the *dates* of these crowns, as affecting their use, it must be borne in mind that the style of the *decoration* fixes that of the crown, and not the date of the wearer (if any). I mean that supposing we are placing a shield on the wall of a Church, which bears a crown for S. Edward the King, or S. Edmund, it is a piece of puerile purism to say it must be *very* early, for he lived long ago. It is the saddest part of the decorative purist's character that he is so like most other purists—hideously inconsistent. Having, for instance, insisted that S. Edmund must have a tenth century crown, he is pretty sure to put it on a fourteenth century shield in a fifteenth century Church, and feel all the while that the right thing has been done.

At the risk of digression, may I here say, on the broader question of "consistency," that the hardest task I have ever had, in directing other artists, or in restraining the zeal of amateur embroiderers and decorators, has always been to secure the faintest coherence or proportion in style.

I build, for instance, a chancel in "late perpendicular." My back is hardly turned when an astounding altar frontal in nineteenth-thirteenth century style (or want of style) is staring and blazing from the sanctuary; or an "early English" pulpit, or a ghastly organ-builder's "case" is erected without a conception of incongruity or bad taste.

We may put *later* work into an earlier building, if we think it looks well; and in nine cases out of ten we *must*, since to the early builders the later developments of ornament were unknown; but to "go behind the centuries," and force our idea of the thirteenth into other men's ideas of the fifteenth is, or should be, impossible.

But to revert to the purist: get rid of him by all and every means, and realize this, which all mediaeval artists did, that the style of *representation* of an emblem (or an individual) must be in the "mode" of the style employed.

To the fifteenth century artist, S. Jerome should be arrayed in a cardinal's hat of the sort that Cardinal Beaufort wore then.

To him, happily, the style he had to employ was his own and every one's else. His medium was the "spirit of the day." For us, alas! who, from our too wide knowledge, have *no* style, we can only go back to such a one as is thought to be the best to employ in each case; but, having done so, we must adhere closely to it, and not rack our brains to think what sort of crown or vestment S. Edmund or S. Hugh wore, but give *a* crown or *a* vestment, the best we can draw.

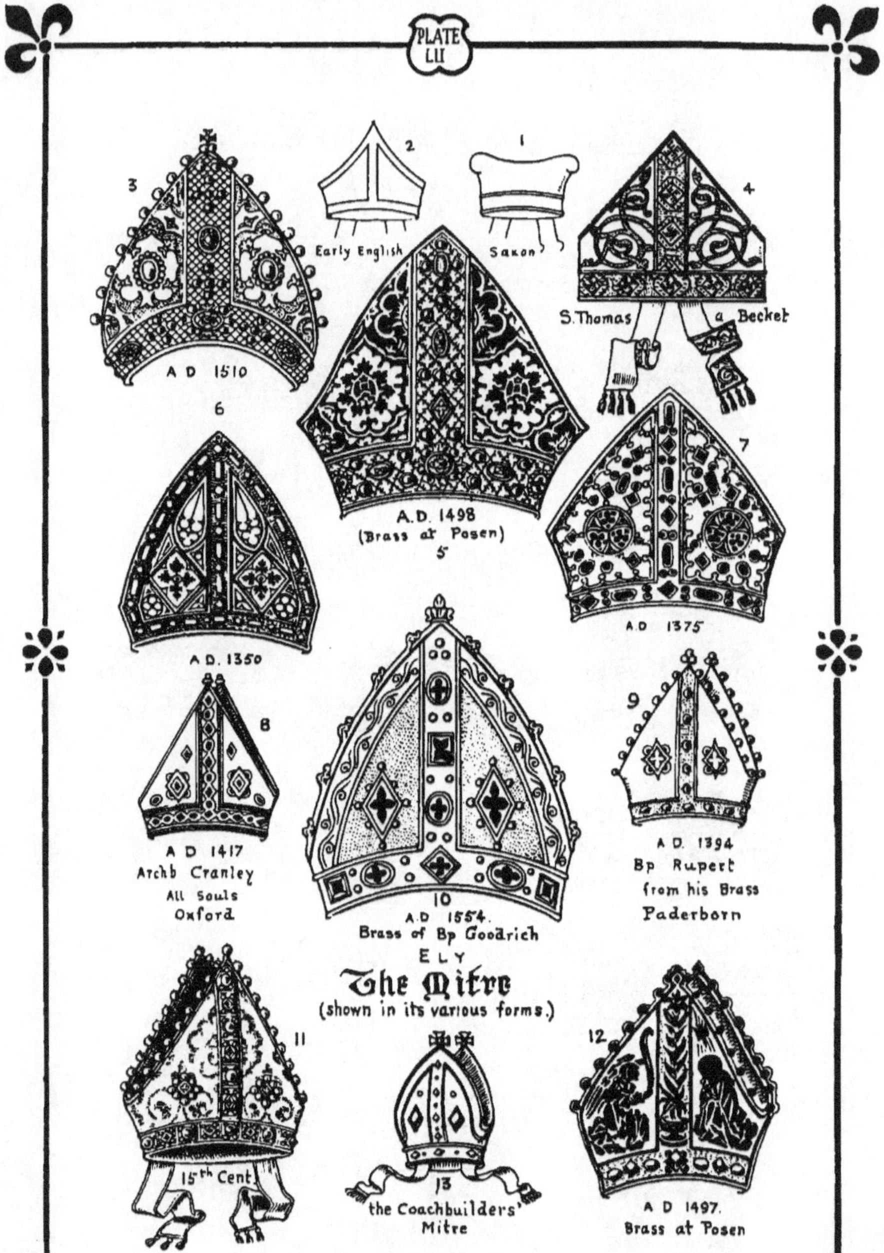

PLATE LII

3 — A.D. 1510
2 — Early English
1 — Saxon
4 — S. Thomas a Becket
6 — A.D. 1498 (Brass at Posen) 5
7 — A.D. 1375
8 — A.D. 1417 Archb Cranley All Souls Oxford
10 — A.D. 1554. Brass of Bp Goodrich ELY
9 — A.D. 1394 Bp Rupert from his Brass Paderborn

The Mitre
(shown in its various forms.)

11 — 15th Cent
13 — the Coachbuilders' Mitre
12 — A.D. 1497. Brass at Posen

CHAPTER XXVI.

The Mitre,

may, perhaps, be accounted the ecclesiastic's crown, since he who has reached this, has nought higher in dignity to attain on earth.

On Plate LII. are twelve examples of old mitres of varying shapes and degrees of richness, and one modern abortion, fig. 13.

The shape of the mitre was originally low and flat, probably not greatly different from that worn by the heathen, or by the Jewish priests of the Tabernacle. To establish an exact continuity between any of the Mosaic and the Christian vestments is a task which has often been attempted, but with success of the doubtfullest measure.

For decorative purposes I think we may be quite content to take the mitre as we find it in mediaeval art—a pointed, cleft cap, enriched with jewels or embroidery.

Its early Saxon shape is shown on fig. 1. Its normal shape during the twelfth and thirteenth centuries may be taken as that drawn on fig. 2, though the lines were generally straight, and not curved.

Fig. 4 is a drawing of the actual mitre of S. Thomas à Becket, still preserved at Sens. As the time went on, each century saw the elevation of the mitre growing little by little, until it attained its full height, in the fifteenth century; see figs. 8, 11, and 12.

The convex outline, generally stigmatized as "debased," cannot in fairness be so called, since many early examples show it, noticeably fig. 6 (of the fourteenth century). The exaggerated curve in figs. 3 and 10 is, however, a sign of the beginning of the end, reached in the seventeenth and eighteenth centuries, when something approaching the coachbuilder's mitre (fig. 13) was actually to be seen on living heads.

The mitre preserved at New College, Oxford, as that of William of Wykeham, has, unfortunately, lost a great part, not only of its ornament, but of its substance. If, however, we may suppose that the dotted lines on the figure below show its *original* size, we have here another good example of the normal shape of the old English mitre.

MITRE OF WILLIAM OF WYKEHAM

Technically, there are three sorts of mitres:

(*a*) The *mitra simplex*, of plain linen, with very slight enrichment.

(*b*) The *mitra aurifrigiata*, of cloth of gold; or white silk, embroidered. Such a one is that of S. Thomas, shown on fig. 4.

(*c*) The *mitra preciosa*, enriched with jewels, and goldsmith's work.

The last-named is the one commonly shown in effigies or pictures of the saints, and the one most suitable for heraldic or decorative use.

☩

Lector aspice finem,

☩

Vale.

☩

www.ingramcontent.com/pod-product-compliance
Lightning Source LLC
Chambersburg PA
CBHW031813220426
43662CB00007B/627